HALF BUT WHOLE

HALF BUT WHOLE

Reflections Of A Twin's Life

Hank Albert

Half But Whole
Reflections Of A Twin's Life

©2022 Hank Albert

ISBN: 978-1-66783-257-9

CONTENTS

Preface

During the summer of 2016, after spending two days together trying to solve all of the world's problems and many of our personal ones, my dear friend Judith said to me, "You know Hank, you should write a book."

I had no idea why she would make such a bizarre and surprising statement, so I answered, "Why should I write a book?" Judith responded, "Because you have good stories to tell."

I had never before realized that that was a part of my personality, but Judith did help me notice that I did, indeed, like to tell stories. But I certainly didn't believe they belonged in book form. And besides, since I was retired, I had become too distracted by my plans to travel, my political volunteering, and my young childrens' soccer careers. I had no time to write a book, even if I knew to which stories Judith was referring. I filed her comment as a compliment, and quickly forgot it.

Two years later, I heard the end of an interview on public radio, in which a woman was being interviewed about her research regarding data and attitudes of identical twins. The researcher had just announced that what most identical twins are fearful of is losing their twin sibling. Being a person who was born with a twin myself, I was very interested in knowing more. I contacted that researcher the next day, and was soon interviewed as part of her work. After that interview, I was beginning to feel myself as being a part of a larger story.

Sometime at the end of 2019, I was considering in which courses I might want to enroll at Temple University's, non-credit, Life Long Learning Society in Ambler, PA. I noticed a listing being offered on how to write a memoir. Well, Judith had suggested that I was an interesting storyteller. Perhaps learning to write a memoir might be a useful tool.

Upon beginning the class, I learned three things. I enjoyed the writing process and the outlet for my thoughts and ideas. The Writing instructor was very helpful and facilitating. The writing process was forcing me to focus heavily and deeply on my relationship with my identical twin.

This focus on my twin-ship has now evolved into this memoir about my life with my brother Chuck.

My friend Judith is pleased that she has found it to be an interesting story.

Hank Albert
Elkins Park, PA
2022

Dedication

This book is dedicated to and in honor of Chuck

The muse of my life

Who shared the womb

Who cleared my path

Who inspired my action

Who taught me courage

Who offered me strength

Who gave me wisdom

Who loved me unconditionally

And who provided what was necessary to complete this project

Acknowledgments

Having never published anything greater than an article on an editorial page, I had not even fantasized about being an author. When my friend Judith Altman suggested one evening that I "write a book" I was flattered, but quite puzzled. She saw something in me that I had not. If she had not made that suggestion, I doubt that this story would have ever emerged. Thank you Judith.

I had never met Dianna Marder when she was about to conduct a series of classes to teach beginners how to write a memoir. Having noticed her in a course catalogue, I was intrigued. I wondered if I could respond to Judith's suggestion about writing a book, if I first learned HOW to write one.

When the classes began, Dianna was a nurturing facilitator for me. My understanding quickly merged with my enjoyment of the writing process, and with my appreciation of her patience and encouragement. Suddenly I was developing a fantasy of writing that book, and it seemed that something deep inside me knew the topic. My hidden pieces were falling into place. Thank you Dianna.

Once I actually began to write about my brother, it was very difficult to stop. I was apprehensive about the quality, but my product seemed most important. When I returned to Dianna for advice, she suggested that she work with me to create a readable and interesting text. She provided vital organizational and editorial support that gave me the confidence to proceed. I would not have been able to accomplish that without her guidance. So, thank you again Dianna, and for your friendship.

When my first draft was completed, I found Susan Adler, a previous reviewer of professional journals and an accomplished editor of numerous PhD dissertations. Susan was instrumental in helping me dot all of the i's and cross all of the t's correctly. Her sound advice helped me give the text a gentler flow and a more understandable composition.

My cousin Bob Chanin helped me find Susan Adler. He also provided expert proofreading of the text that gave me confidence that I had created a worthy document.

Finally, I must acknowledge my wife Emma Raymont and my two children, Cory and Peri Albert. Not only are they the main audience to whom I targeted this writing, but they had to tolerate my up-and-down personality foibles (even more than usual) as the story evolved. I thank them for their patience and understanding. If it weren't for them, I would not even have wanted to begin this project. Thank you family!

WHAT IT'S LIKE TO BE A TWIN

When people ask me what it is like to be a twin I purposely give the wrong answer. I nearly always say, "Well, I have no idea what it is like NOT to be a twin." I choose to be disingenuous, because the truth is much more intimate and complicated. However, here is the story of what happened at Robbie's house:

When we were about age 15, my identical twin, Chuck, and I were with about ten friends on a Friday night, sitting in the backyard at our friend Robbie's house. Toward the end of the night, three unknown boys wandered by, picking a fight. They clearly were under the influence of something they should have avoided. Perhaps they focused on me because at 5'5" I was the shortest. I was nervous but I refused to back down. Even as one of the thugs took a hefty wild swing at me, I felt a surge of confidence, as though I had a secret weapon and I expected something good to happen. At that moment, without a word or signal, I watched as my amazing twin brother flung himself through the air and landed on my adversary with a protective shout. Together, we chased the three of them down the block, never to be seen at Robbie's house again.

In a nutshell, that is my answer to what it is like to have and to be an identical twin.

Officially, I was Henry and my brother was Carl. At about 5 years old, my older sister Sheila declared us to be Hank and Chuck. From then on I was often called 'Chuck' or 'Twinny' or 'hey you.' When we were together, many folks who couldn't tell us apart would deflect their embarrassment by calling us Huck and Chank, or Chank and Huck. After a while we were no longer annoyed by this situation. Chuck and I were very aware of how much we looked alike. I've been told over and over by many family members and friends that Chuck and I looked exactly the same when we were infants. It seemed to most people who met us as babies that we were carbon copies of each other. So why and how could it have occurred that I was born with a tiny little pimple of a birthmark on my left ear lobe that Chuck did not have? I do not know the answer to that question, but that is what happened. And it saved Chuck and me from being the twin who might have been fed twice, bathed twice, been diapered twice, etc. - or not at all.

As infants, Chuck and I both had lovely blonde ringlets of hair. So there were no clues in our coifs as babies that permitted adults to know who was who. But as we grew into toddlers, it became clear that we had natural parts in our hair. Chuck's was the more common location for a part, at least at that time - on the left. My part was the mirror of Chuck's - on the right side. Mirror image twins are not an actual category of twins, such as monozygotic (twins from the same fertilized egg) or fraternal twins (each from separate fertilized eggs). It simply means that they have some features that seem to be asymmetrical, or opposite of each other's. This might occur with hair parts, dimples, or other facial features.

Throughout our elementary school years, I was almost never placed in the same class with Chuck. Avoiding the additional opportunity for us to be competitive with each other was probably a very good idea – for us, as well as for the teachers. They would not be able to call us by the incorrect name if they had never met the opposite twin. But during those years there was another helpful but annoying circumstance emerging.

Just as it was with the rest of our bodies, the way our mouths and teeth were developing was precisely the same. Neither of us developed the two teeth to either side of our two front teeth on the top of our palates (lateral incisors). But, although both of us were developing spaces between our teeth and would soon need braces, the space between the two front teeth eventually became slightly wider in my mouth. If people could remember which one had the wider space, they could easily tell which twin that was by asking us to ...SMILE...

Especially at summer camp where activity and playmates were con-stantly changing, we were consistently bombarded with requests to ... SMILE... followed by the guessing game: You're Hank, right?

But as we grew, even I noticed differences in our twin-ship that made me wonder how we could be identical. Every year at our physical exam before going to summer camp I discovered that I was still about a quarter of an inch taller than Chuck and a pound or two heavier. Shouldn't we have had the same measurements? Why was it that he could throw a baseball much farther (and straighter) than I could? Why did he have a more pleasant singing voice than I did? These are all characteristics that are determined by our genes, or so I thought. Shouldn't they be the same for both of us?

As is, of course, the case with all twins, no matter how much they look alike, they are not the same person. Every person, no matter how much they look similar to someone else, has his or her own personality. And so it was, that no matter how much Chuck and I looked alike when we were young, the best way for anyone to see the differences between us was to interact with (at least one of) our personalities. I discuss more later about those differences and how they might have developed. I promise that Chuck and I were very different people.

OUR HOUSE

When Chuck and I were born, our parents and two sisters were living on Girard Avenue in West Philadelphia in the apartment above my maternal grandfather's barbershop. After a brief stay in a house on near-by Poplar Street, we moved again to our Wynnefield home when Chuck and I were just past our fifth birthdays in January of 1955. We lived in that house until well after high school graduation. During those years we attended Wm. Mann Elementary School, Beeber Jr. High, and Overbrook High School.

The move to Wynnefield happened just before I started kindergarten. The house was on Montgomery Avenue. It was a row house, attached to nearly 40 other homes that made their way down the block. It had three bedrooms, and the six of us shared one bathroom (except for the extra toilet in the basement, which was much too scary to even think about using). The house had a small front lawn and no playroom or back yard.

Fortunately, the back of the house opened onto a driveway where the milkman delivered bottles of milk with the cream still clogging the top and where the trash men emptied the metal cans into their truck. This driveway was one of the three that connected into a huge triangle bordering a wonderful old sandy dirt lot. This dirt lot was our haven, where tons of kids, including Chuck and I spent 15 years of childhoods, playing, learning, fighting, exploring, creating and becoming the people that we would become in the next stage of our growing up. Looking back at those campfires, punchball games, peach tree climbing, etc., we probably learned as much on that dirt lot as we did in school.

Chuck and I shared a small bedroom on the second floor of that house. We usually got along well, but there were some moments when it was much more difficult to share that space than it had been to share the womb. In all, I believe that that room served as each other's first nest; testing what life was like without 'him," and coming back together often to report and to share.

We were usually so invested in each others adventures, that it sometimes seemed as though we were both living two lives at once.

As we grew, our mother began giving us opportunities to develop our own identities separate from our twin-ship. She would buy us the same shirt, but in different colors, for instance. Chuck was the one that clearly worked hard to develop that theme further. He taught himself to play the guitar, which was quite an accomplishment. I didn't. He would choose an author, and read every book that that author wrote. Then he would go on to a different one - another major accomplishment. He saved money systematically. I didn't. It seemed to become important to him that he had the discipline to grow and maintain a small bank account. It seemed to offer him a sense of control and power that he needed at that time. These were all little tricks to help him define who he was, separate from me –separate from our twin-ship. And it may have been a way to validate his positive self-image. I didn't have the need to do that yet, despite the fact that I was jealous of his work ethic and all of his jobs-well-done. I was grateful that he was helping both of us create our separate personalities, but I was too lazy to help. Besides, he was doing a great job for both of us.

The idea that Chuck was competing with me has been a constant unresolved nagging question within me for decades. I do not remember consciously competing with him (other than in the usual games and contests in which all children participate at times). I sincerely believe that Chuck competed more with himself, trying to meet his own standards, to be separate from me, and perhaps to win my father's acceptance. (My mother's acceptance did not have to be earned, it was always available and obvious to all of us.)

I could sense the growing differences in our paths. But underneath, and despite these efforts, we both somehow knew that we were totally bound together, and always would be. This security offered me a sense of groundedness and confidence that may be unmatched. (Is it present in all identical twins? I don't know.) I was comforted by it. But Chuck seemed often to be unsettled within himself, unable to find gratification and peace.

Most of our time during those years was spent on the large dirt lot behind our houses. There were lots of other kids to play with on those three streets and from the surrounding neighborhood. Since the backs of the three streets were facing each other, they formed an enclosed area unseen by the rest of the city. It formed a perfect place for little kids to play ball, dig pits, build forts, get filthy dirty, and still hear their parents call them home for dinner at dusk. Many of our parents could even see us from their windows or back porches. They all took care of all of the kids. We always felt totally safe. It was a wonderful place to grow up! Until one day when that security was broken.

MY FIRST FEAR OF LOSING HIM

Our street in Wynnefield (still) has about 40 fully connected brick homes on each side of the street that totally face the 40 on the other side. They were built in the early 1920's. Montgomery is a narrow thoroughfare on that block, but cars are permitted to park on both sides, forcing it to be designated a one-way street from east to west. With so many families living on such a small street, parking the car was always a challenge, despite the fact that, in those days, most families only had one car. Also in those days, and in that safe neighborhood, no one needed much supervision - even if they were only 7 years old. None of the children needed to go far from home to find playmates or healthy wholesome activity to keep them occupied. Most families knew each other's names and faces. The proverbial 'village' took care of its members when necessary, but there was usually not much need. It was usually a very safe and healthy place to grow up.

Despite this, on one typical early summer night, my sister Bevy was taking care of us. I don't know where my parents were, but they were definitely not at home. I was sitting on the front steps that led up to our front door. I didn't know where Chuck was, or what he was doing.

Suddenly, Bevy noticed another boy running up the street towards us. He was yelling about an accident and that we should come with him quickly. Bevy made me stay at home as she hurried down to the other end of the long block. I waited, not knowing if I should feel excited about some adventure happening, or scared that something bad had occurred.

Soon an ambulance came loudly from around the corner and rumbled nearly all the way down the street with its red lights flashing. At almost the same time, my parents arrived home and I told them where Bevy had gone. Before they could go to investigate, Bobby, the street-wise-know-every-thing member of our neighborhood, came with the devastating news. My identical twin brother Chuck had run out into the street from between two parked cars while not looking during the game of 'Chase,' and was hit by an on-coming car. And in a flash of a second, it seemed as though the car must have collided with me also. I felt as though I had been struck as well.

I could remember nothing after that because there was nothing to remember. Everything in my world seemed to not exist, except the unknown. I became numb – even my brain. I didn't know what it meant. I was unable to function, or even think. Was my brother erased? Was he gone? Did he still exist? Did I still exist?

Fortunately and quickly, I felt my mother's arms close around me. She kept trying to say reassuring words, but the sound of her shaky voice only left me feeling less sure.

Three hours later the telephone rang. Mom and Dad called from the hospital. Next I remember Bevy trying to help me understand the word 'unconscious.'

But at least I was beginning to understand that Chuck was alive. He hadn't deserted me. When Mom and Dad finally arrived home I heard more disturbing news. Although Chuck was not getting worse, he was asleep and could not be woken up. The doctors were not sure how long that would last. He would certainly be in the hospital until he returned to normal, but that might take a while. All of this information was hard to understand. I was only used to things being pleasant and enjoyable in my young life. I was always used to Chuck being there with me. I was not used to worrying about things. I didn't like the feeling that I didn't know what would come next.

Chuck remained unconscious for two more days and in the hospital for more than a week with a concussion. I remember going to visit him one day but he was only allowed to wave to me through the hospital window. Finally, he came home and soon life returned to normal.

As an educator, I like to say and believe that (in some way) every experience is a good experience. But this first exposure to fear and uncertainty had left a powerful mark on my psyche. I don't think I was capable, at that time of my life, of imagining what my world could be like with him gone. But it was my first fear of losing him. The concept had now been planted somewhere inside me. Little did I know then that that experience of nearly losing my identical twin brother would be very valuable later.

Another close call came at my sister's wedding when I was 8 years old. We were in a hotel. My older cousins Karen and Judy tried to convince me to ride the elevator with them. They wanted to see what would happen if they pushed all of the buttons on the inside at the same time. I refused. I walked away, but a minute later they got in the elevator. The doors closed, but the lights on the outside above the doors never moved. We pushed the outside buttons, but still the lights never changed and the doors didn't open. Cousin Bruce started to cry. Mom and Dad came running looking for Chuck. They made me realize that HE was in the elevator with Karen and Judy. Then I got really afraid. People gathered around. Aunt Rose tried to open the doors with her hands. The doors wouldn't open and the lights above them still NEVER CHANGED!!!! I started to panic. I started to cry. I thought I was going to die. Then ….the elevator door opened. Chuck got out and I could breathe again.

MY SISTER BEVERLY

My sister Beverly continued the pattern in our family of having issues with our given name. I don't know when she made the adjustment, but as many people do these days, she changed the spelling of her given name to B-e-v-e-r-l-e-e. But this was long after everyone started to call her Bevy. Actually, I don't remember everyone not calling her Bevy. It was just shorter and easier than Beverly. That's the one I always used. But we all knew that her official name was Beverly – until she changed it.

I have no idea if the decision to change the spelling had anything to do with rebelling against my parents (father?) or not. But that would seem to have fit another pattern. Rebelling against her father was a big part of Bevy's early life.

Throughout her teenage years, Bevy was not happy with the treatment she was getting at home. At the age of 12, her mother unexpectedly came home from the hospital with two brand new infant brothers with whom she became obligated to help. Her mother was an excellent delegator. And although Bevy also had a nine-year old younger sister, it was Bevy that was blessed with most of the feeding, diapering, cleaning up, etc. when Mom was unavailable or too exhausted.

These chores may not sound too burdensome for life in the early 1950's, before it was more common for women to go out into the workforce. And Bevy may have been able to tolerate the situation appropriately if she was satisfied with other areas in her home life. But she wasn't. And the main reason for this was that she wasn't getting what she needed from her father.

I will write much more about this in discussing Dad, a bit later. But what needs to be said here, is that largely to evict herself from this untenable situation, at the age of 18, Bevy got married (to Milton Newman). At the age of 19 she became a mother (Jordan). At the age of 20 she divorced and became a single parent.

MY SISTER SHEILA

Oh Sheila, Sheila, Sheila, Sheila, Sheila! There is a Hebrew word pronounced Mees-Kay-Nah that means 'a person to be pitied' that always comes to my mind regarding Sheila. I cannot help to feel that when she was born she was dealt a very bad hand. She became the 'black sheep' in our family, through no fault of her own.

Sheila was the second child, born nearly 3 years after her older sister Bevy. As she was 9 years older than me, I didn't really see much of her relationship with Bevy. But it was easy to see that Sheila was the second child, and felt like the second-rate child. Sheila must have been overwhelmed by intelligent, attractive, precocious Bevy. And she also received the opposite-of-support from her father who did not know how to express affection or caring. Therefore, she forever lacked the confidence that might have allowed her to fight her way out of the predicament into which she was born.

In addition, Sheila was not a very attractive looking female, nor did she make any effort to present herself as more attractive. With her short hair and the way she dressed, I always thought that she looked more like a boy than a girl. She avoided the competition that often comes between girls by spending much more comfortable time playing with boys – on the sports field, in the school yard, and on the back dirt lot.

Teenager Sheila was a good athlete. She was a fast runner and could catch a ball. When she started to insist on wearing blue jeans and flannel shirts, it became apparent that being a boy might have been an easier choice for her. Mom and Dad tried sending her to 'charm school' and buying her dresses and giving her dancing lessons. Sheila didn't know how to oppose these efforts. She tolerated them and waited for them to pass, only to be found on the ball field the next day.

When finally in high school Sheila met her 'friend' Elaine, and used every available moment to talk to her on the phone (even when literally hiding in the closet), and constantly talk about her, and visit her, did it become clear that she was taking solace in the relationship with a person who would finally accept her for who she was.

Sheila never had the courage to step out of that closet. It made me very sad when I finally realized that she was gay; not at all because she was gay, but because she felt the need to hide it for so long.

Chuck and I loved her. She was the older family member with whom we could confide the most. But she lacked any confidence in herself. She was unable to take any risk. Her first problem solving strategy was to ask for help.

After high school, Sheila's formal education came to an end. She moved from one menial job to another, either because she did not like it, or did not perform well. It took years before she gathered enough experiences that she was able to create a stable enough environment for herself that she could move into an apartment of her own. Eventually, she settled into a position at the accounting office at the Hospital of the University of Pennsylvania where she remained for many years.

Later on in her adult life, when Sheila had moved into her own apartment she developed a friendship with a woman who's daughter became a drug addict. When this young woman had a child and was found to be an unfit mother, she needed a guardian that was willing to care for, and take responsibility for her child. Sheila volunteered to step in.

For many years, Sheila remained the most important and constructive person in J-T's life. She raised him through his adolescent school years, and remained close to him until he could care more for himself.

Becoming J-T's care-giver was the salvation and pinnacle of Sheila's life. Learning that she had skills and assets that were essential to the growth and health of another human being was a tremendous revelation that rescued her self-esteem. Putting them to good use in other areas of her life as well, and helping him through his growth process provided valuable lessons for her, just as it does for any natural mother who raises her own child.

Underneath it all, Sheila was an endearing character. I loved her for her caring, loving, endearing self, and for her struggles. I just wish she could have loved herself a bit more, so I would have stopped thinking of her as a 'mees-kay-nah.

MY FATHER

The first image that comes into my mind about my father is driving him to Dr. Silver's office. It was a cold and rainy night, which is a perfect metaphor to describe our relationship. Dad had a history of heart problems. He'd had a heart attack at 48 when I was only 8. Now, here was I at 18, driving him at 58, because he was having chest pains again. If they were to increase for any reason, it would have been much safer to have a different person doing the driving. It always bothered me that I was the son chosen to be Dad's chauffeur. I had other ways with which to spend my time. But mostly, I wondered if he didn't trust Chuck as much to perform this task. I worry that Chuck may have felt the same way.

Since his first heart attack Dad was in and out of hospitals many times. His heart would finally give way permanently at the youngish age of 71, when I was 32.

Although Dad could be very charming, and was respected and well-liked by many peers, he had several characteristics that prevented him from being revered by his immediate family members. (And I write the following as diplomatically as possible.) First, Dad did not display a great deal of intelligence. He seemed to lack the intellectual abilities that might have guided him to make better decisions in some of the most vital areas of his life. He often acted short sightedly, trying for immediate gratification rather than long-term success and security. Several members of my extended family have even confided in me that he periodically gambled with his money instead of investing in his business.

Second, although Dad owned his own business, the A & B Moving and Storage Company, he was a poor businessperson, as evidenced by the consistent flow of phone calls to our home seeking the money that Dad owed. Upon graduating from high school, both Chuck and I were invited to join the family business, but we could see why that would have been a futile decision for all concerned. Dad never invested in anything, including his business, unless there was no other choice. Frankly, and sadly, Dad's decision-making patterns were often immature and impetuous, made for the quick fix and selfish personal gratification. He and Mom never argued for any reason that I am able to remember except for MONEY. Dad wanted to spend it. Mom needed long-term security. This issue was the main reason for their marriage separation in the mid-1970's after 42 years of marriage. Chuck and I had never seriously considered joining the business.

Finally, and most importantly, Dad was emotionally bankrupt. He was unable to show positive emotions toward, or be an emotional support system for others. This was most obvious regarding his two eldest children, his daughters. This family story includes an anecdote about when he arrived home from work one evening when Bevy, his first child, was just a toddler. She did not, or would not, greet him warmly – no kiss, no hug. Dad decided from then on that he wouldn't offer physical affection either.

I don't know how much validity this anecdote holds, but it seemed to be based in fact. Dad was unable to be close. I was too young to remember Bevy's teenage years with Dad, but I do know that after 18 years living with him, she left home. Later she told me straight-forwardly that she had wanted to marry so that she could be away from Dad. He was not overtly abusive, just simply not helpful.

As for Sheila, I do not remember my father ever hugging or kissing her. I do not remember him taking her on an outing one on one. I do not remember him complimenting her on an accomplishment. Perhaps I was just at the wrong place and time. But these inadequacies should reasonably have been the most urgent puzzle in Dad's life to solve. But he didn't. He couldn't. He was…bankrupt.

Dad was not much more emotional with his sons than he was with his daughters. Perhaps, the fact that he was already 39 years old when his infant twins entered the world had something to do with it. But he was simply incapable of showing his children physical affection.

Periodically Dad would show his love with a gift. When we were at about age nine, he bought Chuck and I a bicycle-built-for-two. But by then we were already wondering if he did that just so he wouldn't have to buy two separate bikes. I do remember the two black baseball gloves we got before entering the Little Leagues. And every few years or so he would take us to the Camac 'bath house.' This was the spa-type facility where men walked around in toga-like sheets and got messaged, played cards, exercised, and had a snack. But a good example of Dad's parenting skills is when he would come to watch us at the bathhouse gym playing basketball - but never say a word to us about it, during or afterward. Silence. He did the same as a Little League baseball parent; sitting on the bench and making not one sound before, during, or after the game.

By the time I had grown into my teenage years, I often wondered what made my father so difficult for me to understand. His father (Morris Albert) immigrated to America from Lithuania and married a woman (named Dora - my grandmother) who had come to America from Russia. He was a short, frail, mild-mannered man and she was a strong, powerful personality. By all accounts, Grand-mom 'wore the pants' in the family. She idolized her eldest son, who she called Jake. To her, he could do no wrong.

Grand-pop originally made his living by pushing a cart through his north Philadelphia neighborhood. He collected old furniture, refurbished it, and re-sold it. Around the time Chuck and I were born, in 1949, he had opened a corner used-furniture store on Marshall St. just north of downtown Philadelphia. In between these projects, and although I was too young to remember, Grand-pop and a partner founded a moving business for people that were transitioning to a new home or business location. Although Grand-pop's last name was 'Kolomitsky' when he came to America, he changed it to 'Albert' so that people who were searching in the telephone directory for a new mover would find his name sooner.

Simultaneously to these events, Morris's son Jack was working as a truck dispatcher. It evidently was a somewhat important job because it allowed him to avoid serving in the military during World War II. Sometime during the early 1950's, Grand-pop sold his moving business to his son. The family had already been able to move out of the barbershop-fronted apartment run by my maternal grandparents to their first house on Poplar St. in the same neighborhood. But only about three years later, in January of 1955, when we moved to Wynnefield, further west, nearer to the city boundary,

Jack Albert became the sole owner of the A+B Moving and Storage Co., and was moving up in the world.

These must have been the most lucrative years of my father's career. Climbing the ladder to become owner of two separate homes and a business in just a few years was a tremendous accomplishment. He owned 3 or 4 moving vans, depending on their availability, in any given year. He worked hard during long hours, including on Saturdays. These efforts would have reaped even greater rewards in the next few years if Dad had avoided some unfortunate decision-making.

My earliest recollection of Dad's business life was when we moved to the Wynnefield house. We had a land-line telephone in our home that could be unplugged and taken to a different location just for privacy or convenience. And Dad had a separate line installed that was the same phone number as the phone line in his office. It would ring in both locations at the same time. We had to answer that phone by saying, "A and B Moving and Storage Company.... can I help you?" Chuck and I thought that was "sooo cool."

The first of Dad's regular offices that I remember was at 40th and Market Sts. It was near Zaida's (grandfather) barbershop in the old neighborhood. But in my teenage years, Dad was running a second company on Germantown Ave. in Germantown called Hoffman's. He administered both companies from the same location. In addition, in order to appease Mom's anxiety regarding the long-term family financial insecurity, he gave her the ground floor of the new warehouse to open her own new-and-used furniture store. Mom was happy to be more in control of her future. Dad was happy to expand his business. The joy lasted a year or two, until it became apparent that Mom was a more successful business-person than Dad. She was making more money. He became upset. Argument ensued. Mom had enough. She phoned a locksmith and - after more than four decades - their marriage ended.

MY VERY WONDERFUL MOTHER

It is probably most appropriate to begin by saying that my mother (like the rest of the family – except Sheila) had a confusing first name. She was born in Kremenchug, the Ukraine, late in 1913 during Hanukah. Her parents named her Paula. But somewhere along the line she changed it to Pauline because she 'didn't like Paula.' But, while working to assimilate into American life as a teenager, which was very important to her, Mom decided that a name like Gerry would be more 'American.' So, depending on with whom she was speaking, Mom was either Pauline or Gerry. Later in her life when grandchildren came along, she appropriately also became known as Mom-Mom. I stayed out of the name-game by always calling her 'Mom.'

Life in Kremenchug had been extremely challenging for the Chanin family. My mother had four older brothers - Benny, Izzy, Jack, and Dave, and no sisters. The family paid no rent, but lived in a house that had no floor, just earth and dried manure, which was put down new every year. The four boys went to school every morning to learn to speak Yiddish, carrying lanterns to show the way during the dark winter months.

After some years struggling to avoid the violence of the early 1900's, Russian/Ukrainian anti-Semitism, and the turbulent political status quo of the times in the Eastern European area, my grandfather Zalman (or Sam) discovered that boys 13 years of age were being drafted into the Russian army. He then decided that the family should move to America.

Zalman left Ukraine first by himself, and was to earn money working as a barber. This departure took place after Mom was conceived, but evidently, before Sonya, his wife, was aware that she was pregnant.

Sonya left Russia for Poland in 1919 with her four sons and little Paula. They lived in Grodna until 1923, when Sonya paid a Polish soldier to take them all across the border posing as his family. This automatically made them Polish citizens.

After other stops in Minsk and Warsaw there were several undocumented stories about Sonya finding refuge for her family in local synagogues and/or working in a hat factory. They did eventually make their way to the west coast of France. It was there that the trekkers were told that Sonya would not be able to board the ship from Le Havre to New York because she needed to correct a serious eye condition.

Benny, the eldest son, decided that the three oldest boys would then go ahead. Their idea was to earn enough money in America to send back to fetch the remaining family and pay for Sonya's eye operation. They also had resumed contact with Zalman, who by now had sent steamship tickets for their journey across the Atlantic. When this indeed happened, their father picked them up at Ellis Island on November 5, 1923, when Mom was 11 years old. She then finally met her father for the first time.

Although I have heard numerous stories about extended family members that had come to America earlier and were supportive, I have never learned exactly how the family settled in Philadelphia (as opposed to New York).

———

Since many sources of information about my mother's early life in America are no longer available, I know relatively little. I do know that she was devoted to assimilating into American life quickly, and not being perceived as being from the 'old country.' She achieved only an 8th grade education, and was embarrassed at her inability to read and especially to write proficiently.

Seemingly, Mom was very social and she loved to go to 'the dances,' sometimes accompanied by a brother, Dave or Izzy, who could also 'cut-a-rug.' I know that Mom married fairly young by today's standards. She was very close to her mother (with whom she had shared a bed for many years on the way to America through several European countries). During some of the first years of her marriage, her family lived with her parents in the previously mentioned small apartment above her father's barbershop in Philadelphia. Despite her strong effort to assimilate into American life, Mom often spoke Yiddish with family members. She used it in our home, often conversing with my father to conceal secret messages from the children.

In addition to dances, Mom must have spent a lot of time watching movies. There was a movie theater on the same block of Girard Ave. as the barbershop. Mom knew who her favorite movie stars were. She noticed styles and make-up and hair, and which actors were in which movies. She had stacks of fan magazines dispersed around her bedroom, and could tell you which celebrity was in the picture on the cover.

I'm not sure about the other ways that Mom spent her time, but I do know that it was not learning to cook. She knew how to make food, but not much about how to make it taste very good. Jokes about this deficiency remained a topic of entertainment amongst her children long after she passed away. To be fair, she made a wonderful chicken soup with matzah balls, then passed-down the recipe, which I still benefit from to this day.

Despite her European-Jewish heritage, Mom was not religious, eschewing synagogue and prayer as much as possible. But to her, Jewish holidays meant 'family time' and appropriate meals. She was very devoted to her parents and brothers, and took advantage of Jewish holidays to often gather one or several of them together. In addition, her mother Sonya, spent several years living in our home during my teen-age years until close to her death. Although it was a major annoyance to us children at the time, it probably benefited us in countless ways. We became care-givers and learned about the virtues of empathy long before it might have happened otherwise.

Bubba, as we called Sonya, was very frail during the time that I remember her sharing our home. I recall Mom having to inject her with insulin doses every morning to manage her diabetes. Bubba left the house very rarely, partially because she could only manage to shuffle her feet across the carpeted floor to move around. It took her several minutes to climb the stairway to our second floor where her bedroom was, clutching the wooden banister with each step to maintain her balance and give her strength. This always seemed quite ironic to me for someone who practically walked across Europe earlier in her life.

Although I was too young to remember the details, I know that Uncle Dave (Mom's brother #4) lived in our home for a short time during a period of recuperation. He was no longer living with his wife when she was ill, and Mom nursed him back to health. In later years, Dave also worked at Mom's furniture store after he retired from being a barber due to arthritic hands.

When trying to understand who Pauline (Chanin) Albert was, an important ingredient is the fact that she was quite short in stature. She was never more that 5 feet tall. Despite this disadvantage, Mom was always present. If she was in the room, people probably knew it. She had a loud, even booming, voice when necessary, though she could be gentle as a lamb and tremendously nurturing. She also had a powerful temper, could be quite assertive, and demanded respect, though not usually vociferously.

—◆—

Mom and Dad met when they were both in their early 20's. I have seen residual evidence that my father did possess a romantic side to his personality, but I never saw any of it personally while he was alive. It was rare that I ever witnessed signs of affection between my parents at all.

Nevertheless, Pauline, aka Gerry, became a mother for the first time in December 1937 when my older sister Beverly was born. Almost three years later, Shelia was born, and it seemed it would be a family of four.

The girls grew up in West Philadelphia and attended public school (Leidy Elementary). Parkside Ave. and Fairmount Park were close by. The movie theater was down the street, and the Philadelphia Zoo was within walking distance.

Although it was not part of the plan, Mom became pregnant again in 1949 – nearly 12 years after Bevy was born. Two children had seemed just enough. There was no room for more kids. So (although it would have been illegal at that time) there was discussion of not allowing the new pregnancy to proceed.

But proceed it did. As the months passed by, Gerry, who was nearly 5 feet tall, grew unusually large. By the end of the year she needed help to rise up from sitting in a chair. And in December of that year, the plan for two children in the family turned into four with the birth of us twin boys – Henry and Carl, who soon became Hank and Chuck.

So by 1949 we were a family of four. According to family stories, Dad worked as a truck dispatcher of some importance, which eventually prevented him from serving in WW-II. The point here is that although the family had little financial resources, Mom made sure to have the time to stay at home with her children.

Although it was always simply by the seat-of-her-pants, and sometimes by accident, Gerry Albert was a wonderful mother – the kind that any child would feel blessed to have had. It is not easy to understand this at first – even from this writer's point of view. But it takes only a bit of focus on the details to really comprehend it.

Firstly, as a very young child, Mom had escaped from her native culture where she lacked everything necessary for a healthy up-bringing, other than a close family. The struggles of navigating her way across Europe from one strange country to the next, not being proficient in the languages that she used to communicate, having no friends when she arrived at any stop-over points, having little to no schooling, and having never met her father, could easily have become much too difficult to tolerate. Having to assimilate into a new overwhelming environment as a teenager in America without peer support systems must have been a tremendously burdensome challenge at times. Having little education, a noticeable foreign accent that instantly made her an outsider, no female siblings, even a diminutive body frame, were all obstacles that could have forced her to find a nice cave in which to hide.

However, what seems to have happened instead is that Mom turned these challenges into strengths. She developed a determination and a power that let her thrive here in her new environment. She maintained a staunch persona evidenced by a constantly productive demeanor. This must have allowed her positive self-image to guide her behavior. It seems that each small accomplishment must have offered her the confidence necessary for meeting the next one.

As mentioned earlier, Dad was not close to his daughters. As his wife did, the girls suffered for this inadequacy their entire lives. But fortunately, Mom was just the opposite. I suppose that being physically close to your children is what Mom learned most from her mother. Spending the first 12 years of someone's life vagabonding through Europe while sleeping somewhere in their mother's bed each night certainly could have an influence on how one raises their own children. She was tremendously full of hugs and kisses and warmth and comfort. Touching was not just comfortable, but matter-of-fact. She showed her caring and affection in every healthy way, and gave her children no room for questions about her caring and love for them.

By all accounts that I have ever heard, Chuck and I were easy, healthy, and very well behaved children. Mom told the story of us finding each other in our separate cribs at 4 months old, and being inseparable thereafter. Bevy, at 12 years old was able to assist regularly with the jobs of feeding and cleaning us, but Mom was the one passing out the emotional necessities that allowed us to be, and feel, safe. If early trusting of one's environment is indeed vital to a healthy and stable childhood, Mom was the nurturing agent that allowed Chuck and me to have that great start. And she had to compensate for the lack of closeness that was manifested in all of our relationships with Dad.

In addition, when we were only 8 years old (and by then Bevy was married and out of the picture,) Dad had his first of several heart attacks. He spent long periods of time in and out of hospitals as Mom served as a single parent. Sheila was there to help at times, but it was Mom who provided the emotional support, discipline, role modeling, and everything else necessary to manage the family. During the next few years, Mom even had to help Sheila deal with her own sexual-identity questions and with bringing her own aging mother into our home to live with us. She really was a powerful yet tremendously nurturing little woman – and (especially for an uneducated person,) a wonderful mother.

CAMP GALIL

When Chuck and I were no longer permitted to attend Camp S.G.F. in the spring of 1960 after being campers for the previous two summers, our parents searched for an alternative summer camp. Our father had returned to work and to good health after suffering a heart attack, so we no longer qualified as a family that needed financial assistance. Being active in our local synagogue, he was able to procure partial scholarships for us to attend Camp Galil. Thus, our lives took a pivotal and momentous turn onto an incredibly consequential and life-altering path.

Chuck and I were campers at Camp Galil for six summers in the early 1960's, from ages 10 to 16. Our experiences there, physical, social, and intellectual, were definitely the most formative of both of our lives. For twenty-four hours each day for eight weeks, Galil offered programmed and serendipitous activities that caused and/or helped children learn, grow, and become.

Camp Galil was only an hour automobile ride from our home, and is located in Bucks County, PA. It was, and still is, a secular, but Labor Zionist oriented summer camp. It stresses the connection between Israel and Judaism, the virtues of communal living, physical labor, democracy, leadership training, creativity and having fun. Kids from ages 8 to 15 are campers, after which leadership opportunities lead to becoming counselors first, and then coordinators of all activities and operations – all before the age of 22.

The folk songs we sang there helped us understand how the world around us might be perceived. The Hebrew lessons, through which we suffered, taught us to communicate in a foreign language and connect with our heritage. The communal living system we used helped us learn about democracy, sharing, empathy, and being sensitive to the needs and points of view of others. The soccer games we played and work (labor) that we did, taught us that solving problems might be easier in a group setting rather than individually. And we learned that by living and sharing these joys and responsibilities, it was much easier to tolerate the differences in people's attitudes, behaviors, and personalities, and to celebrate those differences.

Even kitchen duty at Camp Galil might be used as a teaching tool. Messing with garbage cans, disgusting food left-overs, wiping dishes, putting them in the square trays before sliding them into the conveyor-belt type dishwasher was a coveted job when I attended. It held oodles of stature. I felt that doing the jobs that no one else wanted to do earned immediate esteem in the eyes of many in the community. Then I might wrap my large white apron around my waist, and leave the kitchen for the entire camp to notice. Maybe it looked as if I was checking for any further dishes to clean, when in reality I was planting ideas in the minds of future leaders of Camp Galil, to wonder when they would get their turn to run the dishwasher.

Camp Galil, existed as an educational arm of the Jewish youth group called Habonim (The Builders). The educational program is extended into the school year, seeking to create an intellectual and emotional bond between Jewish youth and the ideological Jewish homeland. So after the summer season, Galil campers are invited to participate in pre-planned activities about once per month to socialize with friends, celebrate Jewish holidays, participate in discussions on various topics and simply have fun. It was in this context, that in the next several years, Chuck and I spread open our twin-ship blanket to include Michael Fellner (and his family).

MICHAEL FELLNER

In 2016, I was interviewed by Joleen Greenwood, Associate Professor of Sociology at Kutztown University in Pennsylvania, as part of her research on identical twins. (Her book entitled Identical Twins- Adult Reflections on the Twin-ship Experience was published in 2018.) During my interview, Professor Greenwood informed me that identical twins often incorporate a third person into their close relationship. I was astonished, because Chuck and I had done exactly that. That third person was Michael Fellner, and it began to happen when we were only ten years old.

Michael and I are still best friends today in 2022, although we live 1000 miles apart. We refer to each other as 'brother.' We end our phone conversations with 'I love you.' We have shared just about all of life's ups and downs – the wonderful joys and the terrible pains and tragedies.

In the summer of 1960, Chuck and I lived in a cabin with about 15 other boys. We had three counselors – young men, only a few years older than ourselves, who helped to make sure we brushed our teeth, made our beds, completed community cleaning and maintenance chores (e.g. picking up liter, cleaning trash cans, kitchen chores, gardening tasks), and did not fight each other to resolve conflicts.

In between those activities, campers were able to enjoy the swimming pool, play ball, learn to speak Hebrew, hike, sing, and participate in any healthy hijinks that would encourage the campers to pressure their parents to make their tuition payments again for the following summer.

Among this group of co-campers was an adorable, tiny, little pip-squeak of a nine-year-old boy – my best friend, Michael Fellner. At first sight, it was impossible to know that that little shrimp could attract such attention. But Michael was clearly one of the greatest challenges the counselors had to resolve. This was manifested mostly by his sassy temper and his ability to spout off inappropriate four letter words. Some of these words I had never heard before, and all of those words I had never used before. Little did I know that being introduced to Michael's vocabulary was only the first of many lessons that he would teach us, which opened up my brain, my world, and my ability to question authority.

Gabi and Werner Fellner, German Jews, who had escaped Nazi Germany, became like our second set of parents. Being different from Gerry and Jack Albert in almost every way, they were a huge part of the awakening and broadening of our perception of the world, despite the fact that they lived two bus-rides away. Michael's brother David was several years older than all of us, but he was always supportive when we were nearby.

I cannot explain why it was Michael that evolved as the extension of my and Chuck's brotherhood, but the triangular bonds existed from the beginning, never to be doubted. Each summer we lived in the same bunk. We shared the same activities and social group to help reinforce the closeness. We truly complemented each other and helped each other grow. We learned to trust and love each other completely and unconditionally.

Perhaps that was the magic. But regardless of the reason, the knots were tied. And when we were in need, the other two were the strong support system. It has been a tremendously powerful and comforting way to go through life – more existentially crucial to me than this sentence could ever express. Michael was with me at Chuck's side later when his needs for comfort and security were at their greatest.

BEING TWINS AT CAMP GALIL

As the earlier story of Robbie's House introduced, being a twin can also contain a unique type of magical power. Once the 'other twin' was discovered in infancy, I always had a companion who served as a security blanket. Chuck and I literally and instantly became 'Best Friends Forever.' From then on, whenever each of us had trouble, there was a (perhaps even non-spoken) support system to serve him. Where there was a problem, there was someone to help identify and help solve it. When there was an unwanted empty space, there was someone to fill it. And when one of us fell down in the mud, there was someone to reach out a hand to lift him up. This powerful magic worked its charms on both Chuck and I over many wonderfully enjoyable summers at Camp Galil.

As we became older and felt more at home and confident at camp, we developed leadership skills that set us apart – from others as well as from each other. During the early years of Galil, I admit that Chuck and I had gotten a lot of attention just for being the cute twins that most people could not tell apart. But soon, we became tremendously attached to our peer group. We all regularly chose to get together outside of camp on weekends. In the Habonim Youth Group that facilitated the Galil environment during the non-summer months, Chuck and I were both offered leadership positions without ever seeking them. And finally, in the last summer that we were regular campers, Chuck and I were both selected to be captains of our separate Color War teams by the other campers. Although it seems trite, and was not an official tribute, we perceived it as a huge honor of…being accepted by one's peers. We clearly felt that we earned these honors largely due to the endowments that came with being each other's twin brother.

As teens, Chuck and I each felt secure in ourselves. Our Galil world was the perfect nurturing environment for us.

But adding this identical twin-ship power, allowed us to experiment and take more risks without even realizing it. It was a secret reserve force to be used only when necessary. It had a most profound impact on both of our psyches. And it will become crucially important later as this story unfolds.

CHUCK'S INSECURITIES (DEATH)

During the summer after grade 10, Galil campers in the leadership program slept in large tents, separate from the main camp, and without adult supervision. One night in the boys' tent we fell into a discussion about the universe, and the future of the earth. One boy noted how the earth is always drifting toward the sun, and therefore, in millions of years, it will melt and be destroyed.

First, Chuck got angry and said that could not be true. He said the boy had been lying, and demanded that he retract the comment. Finally, when the boy refused, Chuck totally 'freaked out', jumped out of bed, and threw the other guy out of his bed while screaming loud enough for counselors to come running to quell the emergency. This was the first episode that began to show me Chuck's fears about death. In years to come several other episodes reinforced this thought. Later Chuck admitted to me that he had feared death for as long as he could remember.

Maybe it began at around age 6 when Bobby Lederhandler threw a toy metal cap gun at me, but it hit Chuck in the head. Perhaps his fears started when he was hit by a car and awoke a week later in the hospital from a concussion. Or maybe he ached for his father's approval, which seemed always to be just out-of-reach. Maybe he was afraid that he wouldn't have enough time to finally earn that approval because Dad had already had several heart attacks. But whenever it began, it was quite clear to me for a long time, that Chuck was afraid to die.

Years later, I found Chuck's journal. The next to the last sentence in the diary said, "I fear death." I often suspect that in life, the more you fear something, the more it's likely to happen.

SINGING

The earliest memories that I have that show the importance of music in our home all have to do with my mother singing while washing the dinner dishes. She sang a sound like a sweet little bird, and made drying the dishes so much more enjoyable. I always believed that she could have developed that talent, but other than at the kitchen sink, we were not serenaded very often.

Sheila also liked to sing. She was a teenager during the emerging 'Elvis Presley' era in the late 1950's. That's why I learned to sing "Love Me Tender," and "You Ain't Nothin' But A Hound Dog" without even trying, and before I was ten years old. Sheila also was a Barbra Streisand fanatic, and forced us all to learn many of her tunes in addition to forcing us to agree that Barbra was the greatest singer ever.

Sheila taught us show-tunes. We learned to sing most of the songs from 'Peter Pan,' 'My Fair Lady,' and 'West Side Story' while putting the cans and cereals away in the cupboards after grocery shopping.

Chuck and I could stay on key, and he was even chosen for a solo in the school chorus's performance of Bye, Bye, Birdie during the seventh grade year. But the importance of singing became much more central to our lives while preparing for our joint Bar Mitzvah tasks just before our 13th birthdays. While teaching us our Torah chanting parts, Cantor Beller, of B'nai Aaron synagogue, discovered that Chuck and I had better than average singing voices. When we put our voices together and sang as a duet, it showed that our two voices sounded much better than singing alone.

When I became an educator several years later, I realized that I was developing a philosophy that working together to achieve a common goal was a concept I wanted to instill in my students. I believe that two heads are, very often, truly better than one. Much later it occurred to me that this philosophy may have begun when Chuck and I were preparing to sing together for the audience at our Bar Mitzvahs. Our voices, when blended together with the other, created a harmonized sound that was fun to sing and easy to hear.

When Chuck and I realized we could do this, singing together happened a lot more frequently. We tried to harmonize while singing to songs from the radio. We bought L-P's from the local record shop. We forced friends to listen to us just for fun. And all of this had a powerful effect on our twin-ship. We became even closer than we had been before. The idea that we needed the other twin in order to be the best we could be - at least when singing – was not lost on us. It acted like Super-Glue.

During the next few years, we left Elvis, Barbra, and Maria and Tony behind and Peter, Paul and Mary, John Denver, Judy Collins and Phil Ochs entered our consciousness, as well as our home. The provocative years of the 1960's dominated what was entering our minds, and music was a lot of what was used to articulate and make sense of it all. As our thought processes adjusted, it was also music that was used to express what we learned and who we were becoming. I do not know why we so definitively developed the same values and political ideas, but whatever the reason, it was expressed in the music that we sang. But one day a big difference did take place. One day before the end of high school, Chuck announced he was saving money to buy a guitar.

HIGH SCHOOL AND AFTER

Despite being a prolific reader, Chuck was an under-achieving student in High School. He disdained studying subjects that were required by the school. He seemed to hold an under-the-surface anger against those that were trying to teach him something about which he saw no value. If the subject happened to be something in which he was intrinsically interested, he was a lot more likely to be successful.

Of course, many students shared these attitudes. But it seems to me Chuck took them to an extreme. There is a very poignant story about Chuck and a particular Spanish test. Foreign languages were not subjects with which Chuck had a friendly relationship anyway. But he could find no motivation to study Spanish at all, other than that a foreign language was required in order to graduate.

With Thursday nights being basketball nights at the gym in our neighborhood, Chuck was going to have to miss the game on a certain week in 9th grade because a Spanish test was announced for Friday. As opposed to studying and preparing for the test however, he developed an alternative plan to pass the test and still 'shoot some hoops.'

Chuck stealthily entered his Spanish teacher's classroom after the school day on Thursday and took the test form from her desk. He used the questions to prepare answers that he was sure would earn him an excellent grade, only to reenter them to the teacher's desk the next morning. Basketball was great that Thursday evening. However, despite his best illegal efforts, being the Spanish student that he was, he failed the test anyway. In 10th grade, he switched to beginners French.

The issue that emerges from this story is Chuck's ability to justify cheating on a test. His angry attitude seems to have been that, "If she was mean enough to schedule a test just after my basketball night, I am allowed to try to pass it any way I can." I am not sure just where this angry rebellion came.

The story also shows the kind of attitude, although extreme, that Chuck carried throughout high school. He was quite capable of much higher grades, and he graduated easily, despite mediocre grades. His lack of effort, at times, seemed almost like a rebellion against the authoritarian system that put requirements on his educational programs.

I cannot explain why I did not have the same contempt for school that Chuck had. I was not angry regarding my school experiences the way he seemed to be. I don't know if he did not do well because of his negative attitude, or that he had a negative attitude because he was not doing well. But in any case, I usually received better grades.

When it became time to apply to colleges, I was accepted at Temple and Penn State – the only two schools to which I applied. Chuck had to opt for community college. He was not any more successful there. After two years he was admitted for his junior year at a satellite campus of Penn State U. near Harrisburg, PA, where they were taking all applicants.

BEING SUMMER CAMP COUNSELORS

Immediately after Chuck and I graduated from Overbrook High School in June of 1967, something occurred that shook us both off of our equilibrium. Chuck and I were told that we could not work at Camp Galil together during that summer as we had planned. The main administrator of Galil at that time, (who I will refer to as G.C. from now on,) who we had known for many years, decided with no input from either of us, our parents, or anyone else that we knew of, to not allow us to work there together. He stated that he felt we could do our best work as counselors if we worked at separate camps. (There were six other Habonim camps in North America besides Galil that offered similar programs.) I wasn't at all sure that we were ready to spend an entire summer apart. Chuck and I had hardly ever been away from each other for more than a weekend. And I surely wasn't confident that we didn't need each other in order to do our best work. Not the other way around.

The injustice of this incident made me tremendously angry when I first heard of it. Not only did both Chuck and I disagree with G.C.'s theory, but basically, we felt that this decision had no merit. Unfortunately, we could never ascertain his true reason. And to make it even more despicable, G.C. said that he had already chosen which of us would go to a different camp – Chuck. I was permitted to stay at Galil.

I cried and argued and ranted and raved, but it was to no avail. How dare he take away from either of us a dream that we had held dear for years? How dare he remove us from our loving peers who also wanted to share this much-anticipated seminal experience with both of us.

But then something unexpected happened that eased my pain. Chuck began to warm up to the idea. He began to see it as an adventure. He began to envision introducing himself to a whole new group of people who had no previous ideas about him. He would be a clean slate. He could have the opportunity to prove himself without any preconditions. He had the opportunity to prove himself separate…. from his twin. And, perhaps he was wondering what the experience would be like if we were separated (for the first time). What an interesting and unexpected experiment this might be. So off he went to Camp Moshava, (aka, Mosh), near Baltimore, Maryland.

Chuck did a great job at Mosh and was accepted immediately. He made many new friends, had a sweet girlfriend, honed his skills of working with young children, and generally enjoyed himself on the job. We shared our experiences through letters, phone calls and stories when we returned home in August. And we discovered that life wasn't that hard living without the other one. Mission accomplished!

I also had a terrific experience at Galil. Being a counselor who is, for the first time, responsible for the well being of fifteen 10-11 year olds was a life-changing experience. Seeing life through their eyes 24 hours per day required a lot of concentration, empathy, energy, planning, organizing, and patience. And I had to learn those skills on-the-job. I admit that I was having a great time. It felt wonderful to realize that I was good at these things. And I knew that I could use them long after the summer would be over. Finally, I knew that G.C. had been wrong. I would have been good at this job whether Chuck was with me or not.

During this time I had been planning to spend the next school year living on a kibbutz in Israel. Having the summer separation would also have made it easier for Chuck and me to say good-by to each other in September. But when those travel plans changed, we didn't need to say good-bye at all. And again, the separation from each other proved that we did not need each other to be successful. More importantly, it prepared us for the greatest separation that we would experience so far.

STARTING COLLEGE

So our two first years of college ran separately - me at Temple University and Chuck at Community College of Philadelphia. During the two years there he accomplished about as much as he did in high school. I took many pre-requisite classes, but I still lacked focus and direction for my studies.

Our father had not prepared financially for sending his sons to college. He had been telling us for years that he wanted us to learn to speak Hebrew and pay for college by becoming Hebrew School teachers. Although it had nothing to do with pleasing my father that is exactly what happened for me. I also was considering the idea that I would like to spend a year living in Israel, so studying Hebrew and learning to speak the language seemed like a logical strategy for completing my language requirements.

In our third year Chuck and I both moved away from our parents, and from each other. We both were growing into more mature and independent young men. I will never know how much that growth was due to the fact that, for the first time, we were very separated and largely inaccessible to each other.

When Chuck began studying about "Alternative Education at Penn State," his life changed, and so did his attitude about his studies. Suddenly, he loved school and he loved learning. For the next two years he only earned grades of 'A,' and he also earned a Pennsylvania State Teaching Credential.

While he was developing this interest in Education, I was beginning my adventure in Israel. My Hebrew language skills did improve tremendously. But my lack of total fluency allowed children to ridicule and humiliate my lack of articulation enough that I shied away from interacting. I missed being with young people so much, that I decided to proclaim Education as my 'Major.' I wrote to Temple University to make the switch, and I began work toward a teaching credential when I returned. So Chuck and I were on parallel but separate life tracks, even though we weren't even aware of it yet. We were about to reach the same professional goal, but arrive there by taking very different routes. This kind of situation is not uncommon in the world of identical twins.

AVI

On July 9, 1969, when I was 19 years old, I was finally on an airplane to Tel-Aviv for a year of study and cultural engagement for a Junior Year Abroad program at Tel-Aviv University – maintaining my student deferment so I wouldn't get drafted. At one point during the twelve-hour flight, I went to use the lavatory. Unbeknownst to me, my wallet had remained on the lavatory floor with three new one hundred dollar bills inside. A few minutes later, I heard someone calling out my name. "Who is Henry Albert?" I saw a tall gangly guy wearing a tie and jacket, with hair that was parted, holding my wallet aloft. This is how I first met Avi Lewinson, who returned the wallet to me with the money intact. Of course, I had no idea at the time that this boy, who turned out to be nearly two years younger than I, would continue to have tremendously positive and enriching influences on my life, and who remains one of my dearest friends.

Near the end of the flight, all members of our group were asked to find a partner who would become their roommate in the dormitory accommodations upon arriving at the university. I knew one person who at least made an honest first impression. After a brief chit-chat, Avi and I decided to be roommates. It was one of the luckiest decisions I have ever made.

Avi was from West Orange, New Jersey – not far from Manhattan. He had recently graduated from high school, was a bit naïve and sheltered, and the yarmulke on his head informed me that he was more religiously observant (a lot) than I was (hardly). When I told him that I was a socialist and also slept sans pajamas, I could see from the awed look on his face that I would probably introduce other concepts to him to which he had never been exposed.

I had come to Israel for a year to learn and grow and expand my horizons as much as possible. Although Avi was pleasant and non-threatening, he didn't seem to be someone that could broaden my parameters.

After about a week living together, I moved in with Paul, from Chicago, who was more cosmopolitan, experienced, played a nice guitar, and had a lovely singing voice. But Avi and I were just down the hall from each other and were assigned to some of the same classes for the next three months. He was not at all off of my radar.

During the rest of that year, Avi and I both slipped into a larger friendship group that also included Paul, (Avi's new roommate) Ira, plus Stuart and Scott. The six of us remained connected all year, and Avi and Ira's dorm room became THE CLUB. This was mainly due to the fact that Ira had a stereo, on which to play Abbey Road and A Bridge Over Troubled Waters. It was quite comforting to be part of a great friendship group while adjusting to a new culture away from home and family.

As the year moved along in Tel Aviv, I watched as Avi broadened his own horizons noticeably. His strait-laced personality disappeared away from the influence of parents. He became more relaxed and more self-assured. He grew an Afro hair style. He bought a guitar and started to learn to play. I still supported him a lot, as evidenced by his attending my "Wednesday morning English class" to improve his writing skills. (During this time, I also decided that Israel and kibbutz life were not going to be on my long-term agenda when we returned to America.)

The six of us stayed in touch when we returned to the states, but Avi and I lived closest together – less than a two-hour car ride. We saw each other most often. He was finishing his schooling and lived in Philadelphia for a brief while – even sharing an apartment with Chuck. Eventually, Avi entered the world of Jewish communal service. He worked for the Jewish Community Center in his hometown, West Orange, N.J. As he moved up the ladder he sometimes pulled me along. The need for any mentoring became a silly joke about times gone by.

Two years later I graduated university with a B.S. degree and an Elementary School teaching credential. As a school teacher, I always had summers and vacations free. During my mid-twenties, Avi offered me a chance to help chaperone a winter holiday ski trip that he was leading for high school aged students. I got to learn to ski and get rentals and lodging at no cost. At around the same time, Avi hired me to be a 'Unit Head' at the JCC summer day camp where he had become an administrator. It was a great summer job that allowed me to return to the east during several of those seasons from my teaching job in Los Angeles. I spent 10 summers at the Y Country Day Camp, working there long after Avi was promoted to higher steps on his organizational ladder. Eventually he was made the Resident-Camp Director in Malibu, CA and later became the Executive Director of the JCC in Englewood, NJ – the wealthiest JCC in the United States.

After all of this time, Avi and I had become irreversible friends. Due to my relationship with him, I have met dozens of other dear friends who are still important to me. We have shared every kind of experience, including life and death happenings, financial issues, family celebrations, and cross country-road trips. We have laughed so much and cried together a lot. We have had a truly un-conditional (platonic) love for decades. By now, that young boy with the yarmulke on the airplane could keep my wallet and its contents, and it wouldn't make any difference at all.

THE YEAR OF ISRAEL - UNIVERSITY

During the year far away, the adventure of being separated from my identical twin began in earnest. The program at Tel-Aviv University was clearly intended to introduce young people to life in Israel. The classes at TAU were all in English. The calendar was sprinkled with weekend student-only excursions to help us experience the country and geography first-hand. The first three months, from July to October, were spent only studying Hebrew language. When we were offered the chance to volunteer for two weeks on an archeological dig in the desert, I jumped at the chance.

Later in the year we had an opportunity to spend two weeks on a kibbutz. I lived in a community called Ein Harod. It had about 500 people and was situated in the northern part of Israel. I studied many topics there, from democratic socialism to how to pick grapefruits. The remaining second half of that year was spent completing my course work and touring more of the country.

After nearly a year away from Chuck, he came to Israel in July to travel the country with me. We spent a lot of time in a Volkswagen Beetle, seeing the parts of Israel that I hadn't visited until he arrived. In one month we more than compensated for being apart for such a long time.

TRAVELING WITH CHUCK (ISRAEL)

Chuck arrived at the Tel-Aviv airport early in June 1970. The song Up, Up And Away by the 5th Dimension, was playing on the radio in the taxi as I went to meet him, and that is exactly how I was feeling. My excitement only doubled as I saw him coming down the huge hall that led from the customs area. After many hugs and greetings, he heard me ask the new taxi driver in Hebrew: "Zeh nosea l'Tel-Aviv?" ("Does this car go to Tel-Aviv"?) And I heard Chuck say, "Oh, thank god, I have a voice again." We had instantly returned to being like the same person.

Most of my fellow students had already left Israel when their classes ended, so Chuck could meet only a small portion of my friends. But I still had enormous amounts of fun showing him my home-away-from-home in my new language. We enjoyed Jerusalem and its history, where we bargained in the Arab market and toured the holy sites. We went to the B'hai Temple in Haifa and swam in the Dead Sea.

The final excursion was a plan to rent a car and travel around the north part of the country for a few days so I could show Chuck the lush Galilee area. We invited a few others with us to share expenses and gas money. Unfortunately, none of them could drive a car with a standard transmission (stick shift). Chuck was the only one of us with that skill. And besides, an automatic transmission in Israel was a lot more expensive to rent in those days. We got a Volkswagen Beetle.

On the first night of the trip we headed all the way north toward the Lebanese border. This was only a few years after the six-day war that Israel had had with their surrounding neighbors, and there were often skirmishes and border crossings that caused problems.

While looking for a place to camp out for the night, we began to hear loud banging sounds: rata-tat-tat, rata-tat-tat" and seeing smoke rising into the sky. Then we heard sirens. All five of us had a different opinion abut what to do.

"Let's go home." "Don't drive any more. It attracts attention." "Find a hiding spot."

Chuck decided we were leaving, so he made a left turn at the end of the street. Israeli police were blocking the entrance. They wouldn't let us pass because people on stretchers were being loaded into the back of an ambulance. The home from which they were being carried was badly damaged. The police suggested we reverse direction and drive away quickly. We happily agreed. Chuck was having an interesting first week in Israel, but it got even more exciting the next day.

Since Chuck was the only stick-shift driver in our party, he did all of the driving. But after the first day, he suggested I take a lesson from him and share in the workload. Since I previously had had a lesson or two in shifts and clutches, and since most of our trip was highway driving, I agreed. All was well for a while. While I had sufficient time to make my shifts, I felt very proficient. But when we came upon a stalled vehicle ahead, I needed to think fast. When I tried to pass him on his left, he began to turn left. I didn't have enough room, and smashed into the rear of the car which, I quickly learned, was transporting the chief rabbi of the Israeli Air Force.

Fortunately, none of my passengers was injured seriously. We were all taken to the police station in Nazareth where (after feeling like hardened criminals for a few hours) we were processed and released. Chuck drove the rest of the way home.

At first, I also thought that I was physically fine. But upon waking the next morning, I discovered that I could not even turn over in bed without feeling pain, dizziness, and severe nausea. I clearly had a concussion, although I didn't remember hitting my head on anything. Fortunately, I recovered after only a few days.

Being together again with Chuck was an indescribable feeling. Re-uniting after nearly a year apart was a completely new emotion for me. Sometimes it was tremendously exhilarating to renew former habits, and feelings, and games, and jokes, and memories. Sometimes it was hard work to avoid old wounds and sore spots. But altogether, it was such a joy – and a tremendous comfort that was like having 'home' travel around with me.

After the next few days it was time to leave Israel. It was time to plan and leave for the next adventure. We had spent nearly three weeks altogether in Israel. And we had at least that much more time ahead of us before going back to America. Next, we were headed to Europe.

LARA VS. CHUCK

I haven't mentioned that during the last several months in Israel, I had a girlfriend. (I will refer to her as Lara.) It was a sweet romantic relationship, with boat rides on the Yarkon River, horseback riding on the beach, and sharing falafel in Tel-Aviv. She made the second half of the year a lot more enjoyable than it would have been otherwise. So much so, that we planned to travel through Europe together before heading back to America.

When Chuck told me that he wanted to come to Israel in June, the plans changed. He wanted to travel to Europe with me en route home. Lara and I simply decided that Chuck could join us on our trip. I could not have been more naïve.

When Chuck first arrived, he and Lara got along well. All seemed calm - until he came to me one morning and said he didn't feel that it was a good idea for the three of us to travel together. I listened carefully to his rationale, but soon realized that he didn't have a good argument.

I realized that what he wanted was to have his identical twin/best friend, that he had not spent time with for an entire year, all to himself. He didn't care that I had made a promise to Lara. He didn't care that she and I cared for each other, and that if he convinced me to travel only with him, our friendship (not just our romance) would be over. He didn't care that he was asking for something for which he had no right to ask. He simply didn't care.

I was put in a horrible position. I was going to have to disappoint someone that I cared about and who trusted me. Over the next few days, Chuck suggested to me that he and I had to make up for a year's worth of separation. He reminded me what a great time we have together, and how uninhibited we could be in each other's company. He pointed out how similar our interests were and how easy it would be to plan a trip we would both enjoy. Finally, he reminded me that Lara lived in Los Angeles. Did we really have a future together anyway? Basically, he wore me down.

I realized later that there really had not been any competition. My twin brother was actually like a vacuum cleaner – sucking me back to what I loved, to what I was comfortable with, to what I was at home with. There truly is a power that many (maybe even most) twins have over each other that, perhaps, only they can understand. And Chuck used that power over me. He may not even have been aware of it.

So, I did the most despicable thing I ever did to someone else. I reneged on my commitment to Lara. I sacrificed my romance and my friendship with her, plus any possibility of a future. I felt lousy. I was lousy. But I was helpless.

TRAVELING WITH CHUCK IN EUROPE

Chuck and I made plans, bought tickets, and in a couple of days we were off to Stockholm, Sweden. Stockholm was a wonderful city, and a great introduction to life in Europe. In Sweden, many people speak English, which made it very easy to enjoy.

Back in 1970, Stockholm had just built a new subway train system that was beautiful, clean, and safe. After boarding a train, you could travel anywhere on the city circuit without paying any more money. The history of the city was fascinating. The food was different, but tasty. The Smorgasbord was all-you-can-eat, making it quite inexpensive. The Swedish massages were deep, but exhilarating. We stayed nearly a week and had a great time.

To save money, (and to be more adventurous,) Chuck and I decided to hitch-hike between cities whenever we felt safe. During summer, when the sun sets so late in the day so far north, there is still daylight at 11 p.m.

When heading south to Copenhagen, it was easy at first to get a ride on the major highway. We found ourselves about a hundred miles south in about three hours. Then it began to rain.

We hid Chuck's guitar under a picnic table at a rest stop and put out our thumbs. Being quite drenched, no one stopped for us for quite a while. Finally, a tourist bus pulled over and began letting folks off to use the facilities.

I quickly jumped into action and onto the bus, asking the tour guide if they would take us along. Chuck grabbed the guitar and promised to entertain the passengers along the way. Hearing a busload of German tourists singing This Land Is Your Land half of the way to Denmark became a favorite highlight of our trip.

Late on the second day, we couldn't seem to get a second ride, so we were about to unroll our sleeping bags under a highway bridge. Finally, a car stopped, but the driver said he could only take us a short distance. After only about five minutes, he pulled off the highway. When he pulled into a residential driveway, we were very confused. He asked us to wait a moment, and then he would take us a bit farther. After returning, he told us that his wife agreed that we could stay in the room over his garage if we cared to stay the night. In a few minutes we were being served tea and crackers and meeting his two children. We had not even asked for help. In the morning, as our host drove us much farther down the highway, nearly to Denmark, I asked myself if this story could have happened anywhere in the United States.

Chuck and I remained in Europe for three more weeks. We had student train passes that allowed us unrestricted access to nearly any country. We went to the Tivoli amusement park in Denmark. We decided that Norwegians were our favorite people to meet. We loved the theater in London and the museums in France. We learned a lot of German in Berlin, Munich, and Zurich. We learned a lot of French in Paris, Nice, and Geneva. The Alps were the most magnificent, of course. The concentration camps were the most terrible, of course.

It was a most fabulous trip. But the most wonderful part, was sharing it all, and reconnecting to my brother, my best friend.

CHUCK'S GUITAR

By the summer of 1973, Chuck had been playing guitar for quite a while. He was living in Los Angeles (and by then, I had had a year of school teaching added to my resume). This decision to play guitar was based on more than just music and singing. Chuck seemed to be interested in being known for who he was as a person – not just as a twin. He was more focused on using the poetry in the music to express his personality, his values, and his opinions. It may even have been a kind of rebellion against constantly being identified as part of a 'pair.' This rebellion was manifested in a number of ways, and learning to play guitar – which I had never even thought of for myself – was one of them.

Chuck never took a guitar lesson. He bought the do-it-yourself books and studied the basic chords. He bought the books that held the song lyrics and music for his favorite artists. He practiced diligently how to position his fingers and switch them quickly and in rhythm with the music. He practiced nearly every day. He became very adept. And the guitar became part of his body, part of his personality, and then part of his psyche. He was rarely seen without it – even when traveling. Then, when he was certain that the guitar was a safe and satisfying way for him to help define who he was, he taught me to play. Here's the back-story....

During the winter break of 1971, Chuck, Michael, and I decided that we wanted to go to Los Angeles. None of us had ever been there before. Chuck was finishing his last year of college. Michael had dropped out of the University of Wisconsin at Madison to join the anti-Vietnam War movement. I was about to begin my student-teaching semester to complete my requirements for my teaching credential. I also had procured a part-time position teaching after-school Hebrew at a Philadelphia synagogue. (My father was so happy.) All three of us were ready for a break and to have some fun with each other. A road trip seemed like the very best idea.

Chuck persuaded a friend from his Penn State campus, Richie, into joining him to hitch-hike all the way out to Madison. (Later, he liked to brag about making it all the way out to the mid-west on $.43 - the price of a cup of coffee.) I had to wait until my last day of Hebrew teaching before I could leave, so I took a plane.

My flight from Philly to Chicago was un-eventful, except that it had begun snowing heavily by the time it landed. Flights from Chicago to Madison were then cancelled, so six of us men from the Philly flight rented a car for the three-hour drive to Wisconsin. I sat in a front seat between a business CEO and a union organizer, and listened to them debate American economic and political issues for the entire drive. It was one of the best educational experiences I ever had.

When the four of us were together, Michael gave us a quick tour of the downtown. Madison is the state capital. During the tour we passed a music store that displayed a picture of this new up-and-coming singer in the window named John Denver. Chuck had already become enamored of his music and decided to buy the album. This began a new chapter of how our lives were changed, amended, enriched, and refined, simply by sharing ourselves with each other.

For what seemed like the next twenty-four hours, Chuck played that album over and over and over again. We all enjoyed the new voice and the new style. Denver wrote songs for a universal audience, so we all found something that pleased us. But Chuck was truly overwhelmed. He wanted to 'own' some of those lyrics so much that he decided it was finally time to learn to play them on a guitar. And so his (amateur) career as a guitar player began.

As he had done with book authors, Chuck learned an artist's music and brought it into his life. He found albums and lyrics and guitar chords, and copied them into neatly typed song books, organized alphabetically. He titled each book with his personalized idiosyncratic names such as The Chuck Albert Aren't These Great Songs Song Book, and The Chuck Albert Ain't It Nice To Have A New Song Book Song Book.

Back in those tumultuous days of the late 1960's and early 1970's during the Viet-Nam war, American Folk Music was much more of an influence on society than it seems to be today. There were new individual and singing groups popping up regularly. Chuck was more interested in the Folk and Protest singers like Phil Ochs, Judy Collins, Tom Paxton, and Peter, Paul, and Mary. He learned to play dozens of their songs and soon he had committed most of their lyrics and chords to memory.

After not a very long time, Chuck was taking his guitar everywhere. He played nearly every day, although (as I mentioned earlier) he was not very interested in becoming an excellent guitarist. If he could play the songs he loved with the skills he had learned by himself, he was more than satisfied, especially since he did it all on his own.

On the car ride home from that road trip, we escorted a snowstorm all the way from California back to Chicago airport. Michael left us at O'Hare and headed north, back to Madison. We then discovered that the airport was closed due to snowy weather and we were going to be there over-night. Chuck found a couple of other guitarists and they began a jam. With tons of students, soldiers, and other vacation travelers stuck in the airport as well, they soon attracted a huge group of folks who began to sing along. In a few minutes it seemed that three hundred people must have been singing Kumbaya with their arms around each other's shoulders. This sing-along lasted for hours.

Of course, everyone around him benefited from Chuck's guitar. He sang for, or with, anyone who wanted to join him. It was a tremendous social tool to win him over in small or larger gatherings. And, of course, it helped endear him to many attractive females. Chuck's guitar truly became part of who he was. It was a joy, a companion, and a magnet all in one. And he never had to worry that it would let him down or love him any less. Later, when he wanted me to join him on our second summer trip to Europe, I said I would go with him on one condition – that he teach me to play the guitar. "Tuning up" was our favorite joint activity from then on.

CHANGE IN PROFESSIONAL PLANS

When I was younger, I had never thought about the reasons why I enjoyed being with and playing with children. I always told myself that it was part of my personality that I must have inherited from someone in my past. When I worked as a summer camp counselor, I enjoyed taking care of my charges, teaching them new skills, solving conflicts, and helping them feel good about themselves. Although it was a true joy, and it facilitated such a tremendous period of personal growth for me, I had never thought of working with children as part of my future professional goals.

Over time, and my year-abroad trip to Israel, I realized that working with children was becoming a 'calling.' And so it was that in January 1971 I began my course work toward an Education degree, and by January '73 I earned my first professional teaching position (first grade in Norristown, PA).

Unfortunately, within a few months I was dejected, disappointed, frustrated, and angry. But I was also determined to not give up. If the school in which I was working was a good example of the American system of education, then I believed (and still believe) that we have a very poor system. I found it to be impersonal, where teaching and learning needs to be very personal. I found it boring where it needs to be creative and relevant. I found it wasteful of time, energy, and money, where it needs to be engrossing and efficient. I slowly realized that I didn't want to be a part of it.

Evidently, despite my disillusionment, I was performing well enough to be offered employment for a second school year. But after beginning that second year at a new school with a different principal, I only began to feel worse.

It was about this time that a dear friend, Nancy, sent me a catalog from a college in Pasadena, California called Pacific Oaks. Nancy knew all about my discouragement, and she thought Pacific Oaks might be a place where I could find a direction that was more suitable to my educational philosophy.

As it turned out, she was right. Pacific Oaks is the best place I have ever seen for children. By the time the school year was over, I had resigned my position with Norristown Area School District and packed my bags for Los Angeles.

During the time that I had been completing my courses for my teaching credential at Temple, my brother Chuck, who had had a difficult time being accepted to college, had jumped ahead of me in the unofficial race to professional acceptance and stability. He completed his junior and senior years at Penn State with exceptional grades. His major subject was Education. He immediately completed the first of his two Master's degrees from Antioch College and headed to (you guessed it,) Los Angeles. He had already procured a teaching position, and by the time I informed him that I was headed to LA, he was already in his second year of teaching for Los Angeles City Schools.

FINDING PACIFIC OAKS COLLEGE

Pacific Oaks College is located in Pasadena. It was founded on Quaker principles and focuses on programs for adult students seeking to work with children. I am not sure how it has changed, but in 1974-1976, it offered undergraduate programs for students in their Junior and Senior years of college, as well as Master of Arts degrees for post-graduates in Education and in Human Development. Pacific Oaks also operates a most wonderful children's school that enrolls children from infant and toddler programs through grade 3.

In the Fall of 1974, when I first read the catalogue of the school that Nancy sent to me, I was tremendously excited. Basically, I got the impression that Pacific Oaks was able to provide programs for children that were based on their developmental ability levels (and not necessarily on their ages or grades). The Children's School was largely grounded on the theories of Jean Piaget, a foremost researcher on Learning Theory.

The school was not inhibited by financial concerns. Parents were required to pay expensive tuition costs, yet the school had an extensive waiting list for students who wanted to enroll. Many of the college students earned college credits while working along with the regular elementary classroom teachers as aides to maintain a very low teacher/student ratio.

Each school day was planned by the adults to create options for the students that would facilitate personal and emotional growth as well as academic progress for each individual student. Play was incorporated into much of the day to give the opportunities for students to test their environment and to develop socialization skills. My impression was that the creativity, relevance, and joy that had been missing in the teaching-learning process in my current work might be found in the school at Pacific Oaks. I wanted to find out if that was true.

During my winter recess from teaching, I flew to Los Angeles and had a tour of Pacific Oaks's College and the Children's School. I met with the Dean of Students who answered the questions that I had had after I read the catalogue. I told her about my initial teaching experiences, and how instead of being fulfilling, they only made me more determined to find alternative ways to use my dedication to the growth of children. When I toured the Children's School, I could see how the learning environments were designed to make them child-centered. I saw through the play structures that children had enormous opportunity for growth and empowerment. The more the Dean spoke to me, the more I realized that Pacific Oaks was what I needed to fulfill my goals as a professional educator.

After a while, the Dean and I discussed my interest in applying to be a student at Pacific Oaks. She told me about the various courses and instructors that might suit my interests. She informed me about the requirements for earning a Master of Arts degree. She discussed the possibilities of applying for a fellowship to work in the Children's School for a year, and earn a stipend. The more I heard, the more interested I became. Finally, I asked if I would have to return to the campus for an interview if I decided that I wanted to apply. The Dean's answer made me realize that I was indeed in the right place. She said, "No. I am on the Student-Selection Committee. I feel certain that I can convince the committee that you are the kind of person that we want to have here at Pacific Oaks." In other words, she was informing me that I was accepted as a student even before I had applied.

I resigned my position with Norristown Area School District and moved to Los Angeles the following June. Chuck had been living in a two-bedroom apartment in Santa Monica just before the Los Angeles city limit. His apartment partner, Kate, was about to move away, making it quite easy for me to move in.

As roommates, Chuck and I found new issues about which to conflict – mostly because he had money to spend and I was a pauper. (I did have all of my tuition money in the bank, but I was loath to spend any of it.) But all roommates have issues to resolve. We used them as learning experiences for how grown adults could circumvent minor problems if they remain calm and thoughtful, even if they were identical twins. Most of the time, we were able to do that, despite the fact that we hadn't lived together for several years.

I worked that summer waiting tables in a family restaurant. It was physically exhausting work, but left my mind free to fantasize about the up-coming new beginning of my professional self. I acquainted myself with Los Angeles and Pasadena. I found out that in the Fall I would need to be on campus at Pacific Oaks three days a week, which was a 23 mile and a 45 minute commute. I procured a part-time job as a teaching assistant at a public elementary school in San Fernando Valley on the other two days. I felt proud of myself for being able to leave my home and my friends and family behind to chase my dreams and the things in which I believed very deeply. By September, I was ready to begin my next adventure. And once again, I wondered if I could have been so ready to do all of this if Chuck hadn't been there to support me.

PACIFIC OAKS COLLEGE

My first few classes at Pacific Oaks opened my eyes to a new way of teaching AND learning. The processes used in classes seemed to be more relevant instead of the teacher trying to download information into the minds of the students, as is traditionally used. I felt that these were the student-centered methods that should be, and that were already being used in their Children's School. Two classes stand out in particular.

There was a classroom at Pacific Oaks for adults called the Creative Environments Workshop. We had two teachers in this class that actually were more like "facilitators." They did not necessarily impart knowledge that was supposed to be engulfed by the students. But they arranged the environment so that the students could discover and use their own learning styles.

The students were responsible for identifying what they wanted to learn. The facilitators' job was to help them discover how they might learn it. If I wanted to learn about Jean Piaget and his theories of intellectual development, I could ask the facilitator to teach me about it or find someone that could. If I wanted to learn to use the potter's wheel to make clay bowls, the facilitator could teach me, find someone who could, or perhaps ask a classmate who might have that skill. Since all students in the Creative Environments class were often utilized in their classmates' learning process, the class was always a buzz of tremendous intellectual interaction. If one could utilize these principals in elementary school classrooms, the schools would function completely differently.

The second class that helped me look at the learning process differently was called Group Process. On the first day of class, the instructor entered surreptitiously, as if she was one of the students and sat unannounced in a seat among the rest of the class. When the start time arrived, everyone continued non-formal interaction, talking, schmoozing, getting to know one another. After a few moments we began asking if we were all sure that we were in the correct location and at the correct time, because the 'teacher' hadn't arrived. Soon some people became annoyed that the 'teacher" should be so late to class on the first day. Finally, someone asked if anyone knew what the teacher looked like. When she finally identified herself, she began a discussion about why we had 'wasted' the first twenty minutes of the first day of this class.

When she helped us understand that class had actually begun at the designated time, even though us students hadn't realized it, we started to analyze what our reactions were to the 'teacher' being late. We started to understand and realize that Group Process class might include our own group process.

Classes like these, and others, were evidence to me that learning could have the emotional impact, creativity, and relevance that had been missing in my own public school teaching. I began to develop an interest in seeing how these ideas and methods were put to use in Pacific Oaks's own Children's School.

ADVENTURE YARD

The Children's School at Pacific Oaks College is a wonderful and dynamic learning environment for children, and I had the very good fortune to have been chosen to work there with the K-3 group. Of the 40 students in the class at any one time there were three regular teachers, three Teaching Fellows, and a number of college students. The reputation of the school spread widely throughout the entire Los Angeles area, regarding what a wonderful educational experience it could offer their child.

I could have completed all of my required class work assignments for my Master's degree during my first year at Pacific Oaks. But (as I had discovered during my initial visit to P.O.,) it was possible to earn a fellowship to work full time in their Children's School for my second year. I was tremendously interested in doing that, because until now, everything that I had learned during my classroom year was theoretical. I wanted to see first-hand how these ideas could actually be put to use.

Since I had already been a teacher for a year and a half before coming to California, I was correct that I might be a good candidate for one of the three Teaching Fellow positions in Adventure Yard - the name for the K-3 class. (All of the other groups in the school enrolled pre-school aged youngsters, for which, as an elementary school teacher, I was not interested.) I was to begin my second year at Pacific Oaks as a paid employee.

In California, due to earthquake requirements, schools are built on one level close to the ground. And, because the weather is so agreeable, school happens outdoors when ever possible. These features made it much easier to create an activity-based program – on the ground and outside.

Adventure Yard had large play structures for children to explore, a gigantic sand box with running water in which to build, a wood shop, building blocks, trikes, balls, swings, just about anything a curious 5-8 year old person could want. The school was a buzz-saw of children's play, exploration, creativity, and wonder. The two small indoor spaces were used mainly for quiet reading and games, Math activities, and getting out of the rain. Each child was asked to choose from a menu of activity offerings each day. Some activities were teacher supervised (e.g. wood working), others were more free-play (e.g. sand box).

The three full-time teachers usually roamed around the small-group activities, assuring that everyone was safe and being constructive. The 'Fellows' were responsible for tracking each child to make sure they were completing their required and pre-determined Reading, Writing, and Mathematics assignments for the day. The activities for these subjects were almost always pre-planned individually for each student. No text books were utilized. Every student's progress was maintained at his/her own pace and according to his/her own developmental ability. Age and grade were secondary.

All of the staff members were involved in making the decisions about what choices would be on the menu of daily activities. Meetings to make these decisions were held every day at lunch and after-school. Children became empowered by making their own decisions about how to spend their time. Socialization skills evolved from children working together to reach their goals at playtime. Creativity was nurtured by allowing children to test their own ideas for how they might reach their goal. And student progress was monitored such that it could never "fall through the cracks." It was a unique and wonderful way to attend school.

My year in Adventure Yard was a magnificent period of learning for me. It taught me how efficient and relevant, child-centered education could be. It made me a more confident teacher with a new repertoire of different attitudes and strategies for helping my charges reach success. And amazingly, I had the opportunity to use the ideas that I learned there in my very next professional assignment.

CHUCK AND I BECAME COLLEAGUES
AND ROOMMATES

Prior to the school year of 1975-76, when I worked in Adventure Yard, Chuck (with help from Mom) bought a large house in Pasadena, near Pacific Oaks. We left our apartment in West Los Angeles behind, along with the daily commute across the Los Angeles Highway system. I became one of the six student-tenants to whom Chuck rented spaces, only a five minute drive to the college campus. He was still teaching in Los Angeles then, but as the Adventure Yard year ended, both of our professional lives took a dramatic turn.

In June, we had learned that a private community-based progressive day-school would be re-opening in September as a new Los Angeles City Public Alternative School. Under the new arrangement, the school would be from Kindergarten to grade 12, and the school district would be enlarging its physical size. The school could maintain its creative and child-centered curriculum. Their philosophy would be very similar to what I had been learning about at Pacific Oaks, and what Chuck had always wanted to try. New teachers were now being interviewed who were interested in teaching in a non-traditional format. We both applied, and we were both offered positions. In the Fall, we would be teaching at the Area H Alternative School, TOGETHER. I would teach in the K-3 program and Chuck in the Intermediate (4-6 grades) Unit.

The Alternative School was a dramatically challenging experiment for both of us, both personally and professionally. "Alternative," meant a completely different curriculum for students than in a traditional school. Students were admitted through a lottery system randomly selected from the list of whose parents were interested in the school's progressive philosophy. It was a highly heterogeneous clientele with students from all over northeastern Los Angeles. The teachers were required to fulfill basic standard learning goals, but how they were achieved depended on the creativity of the teachers. In addition, the school was not administered by a principal, but rather by committees staffed by teachers, parents and high school students. The responsibilities were tremendous and the workload was even greater. It was a high-challenge-high-reward job. It was exhilarating, but just as exhausting.

Chuck and I spent three years teaching at AHAS. Many students moved directly from my group right into his. It was quite validating when parents of my graduating students would sometimes request that their child be placed in his class. I must have been doing something right!

At AHAS I got the chance to activate a program that was similar to what I had learned in Adventure Yard. It was euphoric to have the chance to test the things I believed in as an educator. We had motivated students, supportive parents, and a home-made curriculum. For a while, it was a tremendously successful experience!

TIME TO MOVE ON

One day Chuck told me a story about an incident that happened in his class during the early spring of our last year at the Alternative School. He explained that two of his 12 year old students, a boy and a girl, were nowhere to be found when the class returned from lunch. Our classrooms at the Alternative School were actually a series of interconnected bungalows arranged on an asphalt-covered few acres of land in northeast Los Angeles. Four of these bungalows, including Chuck's, had been placed in a back-to-back fashion. Chuck's search led him into one of the connected bungalow rooms, which was only being used to store unneeded furniture. He needed to flip on the wall switch in order to 'enlighten' the situation. Upon finding the two pre-teens cuddling behind a large chair, he said, "Next time let me know where you are." He turned and walked out the same door where he had entered, flipping the light switch off as he left.

Granted this is an unconventional 'teaching style," and most teachers would disagree about its appropriateness. But Chuck explained to me that was sending a message about his trust in those two students. He was telling them he might not be upset every time that they stepped outside the rules because they were trustworthy. And he was telling them that he was approachable if they might later want or need support. (Remember, Chuck was not a believer in always following the rules.)

This story exemplifies why Chuck's students were so close to him. It helps explain why they would open up to him when they couldn't talk to others. It was during those Alternative School years that Chuck learned that he seemed to have a knack, maybe a gift, for getting young children to talk with him about their issues and problems. He had an exceptional ability to develop a sense of trust in them. This skill was useful for helping his students improve their self-esteem, reach solutions, and earn more academic success.

Eventually, Chuck wanted to see if he could take these skills into a new direction. He decided to apply, and was accepted, to complete a second MA degree in Clinical Social Work at Smith College in Massachusetts. He wanted to nurture these tendencies into a second career.

So after three years, both Chuck and I gave notice. I also left California and returned to Philadelphia. I had only remained in LA for the professional benefits, never having made a real connection or commitment to the locale. With my time at Area H completed, and Chuck moving on as well, I had no reason to remain there. I was 28 years old. I wanted to go home to think about starting a family.

CHUCK'S INSECURITIES (WOMEN)

I have a memory of my parents and I walking to a restaurant from our car when I was about 9 years old. I remember Chuck holding my mother's hand, while I ran up ahead, not needing to be protected or supervised. Even at that age, I consciously noted the difference in attitudes between myself and my brother. I noticed that I was happy with myself, and was feeling a sense of independence. I am not saying that this was a total description of our overall personalities. On that particular day, I was feeling self-assured. But perhaps, the fact that he was not, may have been a precursor to some of Chuck's later challenges.

I have already written about how Chuck worked to maintain his positive self-image parallel to me. But when he took risks, (and being the more impetuous twin, he was much better at risk-taking that I was,) he sometimes became less secure, and sought re-assurance. This was particularly apparent when he entered into a relationship with any girls that were more than a 'friend' relationship.

Chuck was attractive, funny and playful, gregarious, caring, respectful and generous. Many people of many ages were drawn to him – including girls. He played a nice guitar that articulated his sensitive values easily, and made him vulnerable in an endearing way. And when he was feeling secure he was a terrific partner. Unfortunately, his insecurities were his Achilles Heel.

Beginning in his teenage years, Chuck had many, many, romantic relationships with a variety of females. None were very long lasting. Usually six months was a long time for him to stay with one partner. He never shared a living situation with just one significant other. When Chuck had a girlfriend, he struggled with the fear that the relationship might end. His behaviors became less confident. He would become needy. He would ask his girlfriend for help. "Please tell me that you love me." This strategy was not attractive and it worked against him. But this pattern happened over and over and over again. And it sabotaged his happiness and gratification.

I don't remember experiencing my twin brother when I could have labeled him confident, secure, or settled. There were times when he seemed to be "uncomfortable in his own skin." He certainly had joyful, pleasure filled, and happy moments and experiences. But he usually seemed to be trying to 'keep his head above water,' trying to find validation. Granted, I prefer to blame my father for Chuck's insecurities somewhat because I worry that it might have been me that was responsible for Chuck's issues. I know that that is possible. But in my deepest heart, I do not believe that it's true.

In truth, I was hardly much more of a success with girls. To avoid being insecure, I would sometimes set my standards too high and avoided many relationships altogether. And when I did get involved, I might have made too many compromises (also out of fear that the romance might end), and sabotaged my chances of being happy. But finally I learned from some of my mistakes. I did find some meaningful partnerships that were healthy and sustained. Perhaps Chuck would have been at least as successful if he had had more time.

SMITH COLLEGE

In August of 1981, I had the pleasure of attending the event where Chuck extinguished many of his self doubts. As I watched him leave his seat and climb onto the stage to receive his diploma as a Master of Arts in Social Work, I was bursting with pride in him and joy for him. It was a culmination of tremendous effort, discipline, and intellectual dedication. It was a job so very well done.

The Smith College Master's degree program is tremendously demanding. Chuck had resigned from his teaching position in Los Angeles a bit early to attend the first of three, on-campus full-summer sessions in June of 1979. The two academic years in between these summers were each spent at an assigned practicum-based program at any of a series of possible locations around the country. Chuck was assigned both times to facilities in the suburban Boston area.

I remember him telling me about a therapy group for single parents, for example, that he created and implemented. The parents very much wanted to be the best parents for their children, but it was often difficult to maintain a steady income, stay healthy, and find time to care for the little ones. Chuck, who had never had a wife or child of his own, was just learning about theoretical family life and the way the real world works, but was somehow able to offer sage advice to others at the same time.

The academic challenge during the school years was also very demanding. By this graduation, I already had known that Chuck had never committed so much of himself to anything else in his life. He had often complained about the intensity of the program, the research, the difficult writing assignments, and the competition with other top-notch students at Smith. But he found the time and discipline to navigate Smith's intensely political environment, participate in a Men's group, and take part in the final series of parody performances for graduation that made fun of as many topics and people as could be squeezed into the appropriate time frame. It was within this process that Chuck became the man for whom he had been searching. He was now prepared to lead the life for which he had been yearning and for which he had prepared himself. All of his family members, including his father, were present to witness this culminating event, and we were all there to rejoice together with him.

On this momentous graduation day, I met several important friends and faculty members. One of them was Chuck's best friend at Smith, Perry White. Perry was to become a most crucial person in my life also within the next two years. And also on that day, Chuck announced that he was moving back to his hometown of Philadelphia to pursue a career as a Clinical Social Worker.

CHUCK AT DAD'S DEATH

I have hinted earlier about Chuck's inner struggles - his lack of inner peace, with which he struggled during his teen years and into his adulthood. I will never know if these issues were due to our on-going and intrinsic competitions, or if his grudge was with my father, who was so unable to offer acceptance and approval to any of us. However…in April of 1982, less than a year after Chuck's graduation from Smilth College, my phone rang. My cousin Suzie Jo was on the phone, informing me that my father had had another heart attack. She said it seemed that if I ever wanted to see him alive again, I had better drive down in Hahnemann Hospital in Philadelphia.

I rushed through stop signs and red lights and highway traffic and made the 30-minute drive in 20 minutes. Many of my extended family members were already there. My parents had not been living together for several years, but Mom was there. Bevy arrived soon after me from her home in New Jersey. Sheila was there and Chuck was on his way from work where he had been working as a therapist in Philadelphia for the last few months.

Earlier that day Dad had been at work, supervising one of his work crews who were moving a family to a new house. His collapse was not the first of his life. After many heart attacks since we were children, there had been several times when he seemed to have escaped death at the last minute.

I sat in a corner of the waiting area alone. I thought about all of the times as children Mom had taken us to visit him in one hospital or another. I remembered times in our living room that we played in whispers, so as not to wake Dad from his nap on the sofa for fear of annoying him into another heart attack. Thoughts of how we needed to 'behave' entered my mind. I would never have wanted to be the one that caused my father's death by displeasing him at the wrong moment. It was not an easy way for a child to grow up.

Now the examining doctor came out and told us that his heart was barely working. This time there may be no reprieve. Many of us waited for hours for some word. People came in and out regularly. Chuck arrived. His agitation was palpable.

It was very late that night when we were told my father had died at age 71. Stunned, quiet sadness arose from everyone, except Chuck. He erupted in anger, pounding his fist against the wall. I will never forget his exasperated and resentful quote, "No, no, you can't die. I'm not done with you yet." We never spoke about it, but I had my own interpretation. I heard Chuck confiding his own unfinished process and desire to still be approved by his incapable and emotionally empty father. He wanted more time. Again, my father could not provide what was needed and requested. And Chuck had no idea how little time he himself had left anyway.

ILLNESS

Not long after Chuck had moved back to Philadelphia in the Fall of 1981, he rented an apartment about five minutes drive from mine, and earned his first position as a clinical social worker. The job was in a depressed neighborhood near the University of Pennsylvania. He told me stories of clients that truly wanted to improve their lives but did not know how. It was clear to me that many of those people did not have anyone else to listen to them. Chuck, as a wonderful empathetic listener, was perfectly suited for the job.

During this time, Chuck also met up with some old Camp Galil buddies who were visiting Philly for the Thanksgiving holidays. One friend brought a rumor that Galil was in financial distress and was in disrepair. The friends decided that what Galil definitely needed was a huge gathering of alumni to go there to fix, paint, clean, and organize. The next day when Chuck contacted the camp administration he discovered that Galil was doing fine and didn't need the helpers. Still, the idea of gathering there with old friends seemed like a wonderful idea. Thus, the concept of the first formal Camp Galil reunion in its history took shape.

Over the next half year, plans for the coming reunion evolved. With Chuck and three other friends working tirelessly as the core planning group, the weekend of October 10th-12th was circled on the calendar. My schedule prohibited me from taking a very active role, but I could see that making plans and finding old friends, was definitely being a labor of love.

In the end, well over one hundred former Galil campers and their family members came to the camp site to reminisce, sing old songs, revive camp activities, and just be together again. It was a tremendous success, with Chuck and the other three initiators taking many bows. Later, Chuck's best friend from Smith College, Perry White, would say to me, "He gathered everyone back together to say good-bye."

It was only two weeks after the wonderful reunion that Chuck phoned me one evening to say that he had the flu, and could I bring him some soup. He had complained to me that he had trouble staying awake during one of his therapy sessions, and all he wanted to do was sleep. Over the next few days he became unable to digest any food. I was feeling concerned and stayed in touch closely. When he started to run a low-grade fever, I was beginning to worry. I called his doctor, a good friend who made a house call, and was told that there was nothing in his system that should be problematic. "Perhaps we should take him to the emergency room to get checked out further." That was the first time I felt the meaning of the word DREAD.

At the emergency room they told us that Chuck had a flu that would need some time to work through his system. They gave him intravenous fluids to overcome his dehydration and sent us home at 3 in the morning. Upon arriving at Chuck's apartment he promptly vomited the fluids they had given him over the second floor porch railing. DREAD visited again.

I left Chuck sleeping in his bed, but at 7 a.m. my phone rang. It was him; but all he could say was, "I'm so sick, I'm so sick." DREAD returned overwhelmingly! After a few words of insincere reassurance I phoned Mom while I prepared for my teaching day. My instructions to her were to come and take Chuck back to the emergency room until they could find out what was actually wrong with him. "Don't let them send him home without an accurate diagnosis."

When I arrived at the hospital after my school day, Chuck was with Mom in radiology having a CT scan. As they wheeled him out, I asked the technician for a report. She said, "You'll have to talk to the doctor, but it doesn't look good."

DREAD totally overcame me. I would have panicked, if I had not remembered that to take care of him, I needed to take care of me first. That was a useful reminder to myself, which I employed quite regularly after that.

At the meeting with the doctor the next morning, we were told that Chuck had had a spinal tap over night. The determination was that he was suffering from meningitis. I didn't understand at that time, the sense of relief that I felt at that diagnosis. DREAD began to disappear.

Somewhere inside of me, I realized that meningitis is treatable. "They know what is wrong with him and they can repair it. It would be long and difficult, but he would recover." I released the terrible thought that I had been pushing down into my psyche. "I would not have to lose what was the most precious thing in my life."

Unfortunately, I WAS WRONG! THEY WERE WRONG! The spinal tap was wrong. As the CT image showed, the picture of the BRAIN TUMOR that he actually had growing inside of his head, was not wrong. The DREAD returned much worse than before and filled my entire being. I felt the tears pouring down my face. It was the first of many, many days that I would sob and sob. Life had turned against us. I had no idea how to fight back. Nevertheless, I did the best I could to care for him in the hospital nearly every day for the next six months.

SHARING THE NEWS

I don't know what physical changes must have taken place within my body after hearing the incredibly devastating news. But driving from the hospital, it seemed as though the windshield of my car was a movie screen, and I could watch life out there on the screen, as I was totally disconnected from it.

Sheila and Michael, had to be told about Chuck's diagnosis and I needed to tell them face-to-face. We were all meeting at my apartment.

They could see immediately that I had been crying, which made the tears flow again. Somehow, the ability to stand erect deserted all of us when I told them the news. It was a completely overwhelming surreal scenario – one that I had never experienced before or after. Life was just a blur.

The mental energy we used up in the next hours was tremendously exhausting and we needed sleep. All of us were too frightened to be alone, and we wound up sleeping on the furniture and floor in my apartment's living room. The next morning there was work to be done. I went to see my mother, who was about to hear that her child's life was in jeopardy.

My other two allies began to make phone calls to other family, friends and bosses. I began to contact close relations to see who could identify the best brain surgeon in Philadelphia. Soon we kept hearing the same name – Fred S. at Pennsylvania Hospital. In one more day we had Chuck transferred there. Good news.

But after examining Chuck and seeing his films, Fred S. declined to be Chuck's doctor. He explained that the tumor was in a very difficult location and trying to reach it in surgery might damage healthy brain tissue. He asked me to imagine separating the chocolate from vanilla-fudge ice cream without hurting the rest of it. The only strategy that he suggested was to try to kill, or shrink, the tumor with radiation treatment. But Pennsylvania Hospital (in those days) did not have radiation capability.

Chuck was soon transferred to The University of Pennsylvania Hospital (not to be confused with Pennsylvania Hospital), which was able to provide radiation services. This is where I first met a most amazing angel of a man, Dr. Leonard Bruno, who took charge of Chuck's medical care. He was a tremendously efficient and effective caregiver to Chuck, and a most empathetic and compassionate manager of our distraught family's situation. Dr. Bruno taught me never to listen to any other doctor or nurse regarding my brother's illness. For the next several months, I came to rely on him for correct information, honesty, competence, and my sanity.

SURGERIES

The first procedure that Chuck had to endure was a biopsy of the tumor to confirm the CT diagnosis. He also had a shunt inserted in his head to prevent cerebro-spinal fluid from building up and causing pressure on his brain. (The shunt diverted fluid from the brain's left ventricle where the fluid was created, through a tube to Chuck's stomach where it was passed out with other unnecessary bodily waste.)

When radiation treatments were begun, they happened every weekday for several weeks. The treatments were painless, but they drained Chuck of energy and made him anxious. And finally, in February he needed surgery again to repair the shunt, which had become clogged and blocked.

The tumor, and the brain pressure it caused, destroyed many messages from traveling through Chuck's brain properly. He was unable to think logically, interpret incoming language clearly, or organize his emotional self. He was confused, frightened, and angry. He lashed out verbally and often physically. Over the next few weeks, medication helped him calm down, but he remained unable to feed himself, walk, or use the bathroom.

Before Christmas, Chuck's condition had deteriorated so much that he became comatose. We were told that his life was fading, and that we should all prepare for the worst. I went home that night thinking that all of our prayers were for naught. But when I returned the next morning… Chuck was sitting up in bed eating breakfast.

I was amazed. The radiation had started to take effect. The tumor had begun the process of necrosis. The dead tissue began to fall away, and the pressure in his head was reduced. We were all over-joyed. Such was the roller coaster ride-of-a-year that we were all living. It was unpredictable, but always somewhere between DREAD and HOPE.

Chuck remained in the hospital for several more months, waiting to see if the radiation had indeed killed the tumor. (Chemotherapy was not offering any desired affect.) As it shrunk, his condition improved and he was attending (with tremendous support) simple daily therapy sessions at the gym. When he improved enough to leave the hospital in the spring, he was almost capable of processing speech patterns. Unfortunately, this was yet another short-lived victory.

PERRY

Although I didn't have any relationship with him at that time, and I had not seen him since the graduation at Smith College, I phoned Perry White, who was living in New York, after locating his number in Chuck's phone directory. When I told him about Chuck's diagnosis, he was understandably crushed. He immediately began to weep on the phone.

I had made this phone call very soon after Chuck's brain-tumor diagnosis. Since the tumor was not yet far advanced, Chuck was then somewhat lucid. He knew he was very ill. If he had any doubts about that, they surely must have been erased when he saw that Perry and Maia, Perry's girlfriend, had come to visit him in the hospital from their home in Brooklyn. But despite that, something wonderful, and at the same time traumatic, happened during the conversation.

While Chuck was lying in his hospital bed, unable to walk, get out of bed, feed himself, or even understand what was wrong with him, Perry announced that he and Maia were now engaged to be married. Chuck smiled. Chuck actually smiled. He was truly gratified. He was shifting his thinking and feelings to outside of his self. For a brief shining moment he was the caring and empathetic person that people loved. He said "Mazel Tov" to congratulate them. Perry and I immediately looked at each other. It was the first time I had seen that kind of behavior in weeks. But I hid my joy from Chuck so as not to emphasize that such a little thing, was actually such a big event. This visit happened just over a year after they both had graduated from Smith with their MSW's.

Perry is a very soft-spoken, articulate and sensitive human being. Talking with him that afternoon at the hospital allowed me to quickly understand why Chuck had become so enamored of him. His having a background in social work must have been a key ingredient that allowed me to feel so safe and open with him. He became an instant ally – empathetic, intelligent, capable, understanding, and patient. These were not necessarily attributes that I could find in my sisters or my mother for whom I was already becoming a caregiver.

Perry became my only other shoulder to lean on aside from Michael. In that first conversation he became optimistic enough to believe that Chuck might recover, although he was realistic enough to know that he probably would not. That was just what I needed. He provided reasonable hope.

Perry and Maia stayed most of the afternoon that day in November. On average they came to visit Chuck (and me) in the hospital every other weekend for the next five months. My family and I agreed that since they were doing so much traveling by train, that we should allow them to use Chuck's car. Months later, to show our gratitude for their commitment to him, we sold them his car for one dollar. Or you might call it a nice wedding gift that next summer to which I had to attend alone.

THE LAST DAY

By the end of April 1983, radiation treatments had shrunk the tumor enough that Chuck was actually going to Physical Therapy sessions in the hospital. Now he could stand by himself and was trying to learn to walk again. I would face him and hold his hands to help him keep his balance as he shuffled toward me. I could not tell if the anguish in his face was due to the lack of success in taking that last step, or from trying to figure out why he was unable to perform this fundamental task. He was such a proud and determined man. Why was he in this position of starting his life over again in such as infantile manner? Even if he could have asked the question, neither of us knew the answer.

Soon, Chuck's health insurance company wanted him to leave the hospital so that they could stop paying for his expensive care and treatments. Miraculously, an apartment became available on the same floor as Mom's in her apartment building. After five months in hospitals, we were now able to outfit the suite with a hospital bed. We hired 24–hour nursing to help take care of my confused but grateful twin brother.

For two very hopeful weeks Chuck was out of any hospital and in the company of his family. He was somewhat cognizant of his surroundings, and was fairly comfortable. I would keep the room filled with music that he enjoyed and Phillies spring training baseball games. We were still living on a dream and a sliver of hope that he would continue improving.

(It was explained that the dead tumor cells that had been destroyed by radiation treatments might continue to disappear for a time, opening space in his brain for healing, possible understanding, and continued clarity. More progress was still possible.)

Unfortunately, after the two weeks home, Chuck developed a fever that wouldn't leave. We were directed to return him to the hospital to find the cause. During that stay, a new CT scan of his head was ordered, and it showed what we had all been fearing - new tumor growth. That same original blanket of DREAD returned again just as it did last fall. We were all horrified.

Since Chuck had already had a full dose of his radiation treatments, any more could now begin to harm, instead of, help him. Any chemotherapy he had had proved unsuccessful. Now he had no remaining weapons with which to fight his illness. Any hope to which we had clung was now baseless.

The doctors were now suggesting that we remove Chuck's medications, allow the doctors to keep him totally comfortable with an array of different palliative drugs, and let the cancer take its course. We had no choice but to agree. There was no need to prolong the inevitable.

At least he would no longer be tormented, agonized, and in misery. That would be left for his family and others who loved him – especially for his twin brother who was losing half of his psychic self. But Chuck would at last be at peace.

Of course it was a most loathsome, hideous, and grotesque decision. It was as if I was being asked to kill a part of myself. My family pretended that they were helping me decide Chuck's fate, but without any words being spoken, we all knew that it was my decision. I was the best person to understand what Chuck would have wanted. It was as if I were choosing what to do with my own life.

And so, somehow, I did. Living like he had been for the last six months was not living at all. The quality of his life was his most precious possession. With all hope for a miracle gone, Chuck would have wanted to end his torture as well as ours. Even though it was a hideous decision, it was the correct one.

During the next week, Chuck drifted into a coma never to communicate anything again. His fever spiked regularly, and he was given a refrigerated blanket to keep his temperature down. The nurses with whom we had spent the last several months had trouble looking at us in the eye, but remained even more attentive to our needs and requests as well as Chuck's. Palliative drugs were administered. Friends and loved ones paid their final visits.

———

Quickly, the ever-present sense of panic and exhaustion disappeared from within me. I no longer had to be worried, now that I knew the certain pending outcome. But…I began to understand that my feelings of DREAD that were no longer present would only be replaced by the guilt that was now seeping into my deepest self. Why had it been my fate to be in a position to allow my precious brother to die? Why did my brother die while I survived? Why had I ever been in a position to lose what was most essential to me?

As I looked at my beautiful, once vital brother lying helplessly and non-existent in the hospital bed, I saw the two of us living our nightmare to its final end. The terrible dream didn't disappear when I woke up, as most nightmares usually do. Instead it penetrated me. It found a resting spot in every part of my self, never to leave again. Not even until this day as I write this sentence.

In late afternoon of Monday, May 2nd, 1983, Michael came to the hospital room. His visits to the hospital had become sparse, although I saw him nearly every day when his parents fed me a 9 p.m. dinner after visiting hours on my way home. Sheila was with me as well. Her shift at her job in the accounting office of the hospital had ended at 5 p.m.

When Michael looked at Chuck, he began to cry. Although Chuck was still breathing, he was gone. Michael didn't want to wallow there, so we went to the cafeteria for coffee. We began to talk about the arrangements that would need to be made, but I felt no strength for that. We exited the elevator on the 9th floor of Ravdin Building. As we walked toward Room 933, Sheila came out of the room. Her red eyes stared at us. As we approached she said, "He must have waited for you to leave. He stopped breathing as soon as you were out of the room."

Chuck died at 6:10 p.m. And a large part of me died with him.

SLOW AND STEADY RECOVERY

How does one recover from such an enormous catastrophe? I discovered that it happens very slowly. But it can happen.

Chuck's funeral was attended by hundreds of family and friends. Many people came from far away. Michael was in charge of piping in tapes of music that my brother loved into the chapel audio system. I tried to think of how Chuck might have wanted each detail to occur according to his preferences.

Unfortunately, during the school year that Chuck had been in the hospital, being the best schoolteacher that I could be was not a very realistic goal. My main goal had been to 'not be a poor schoolteacher.' I remember many times when I sat on the floor of Chuck's hospital room and tried to grade students' composition papers as he slept. While trying to keep my brother alive and as comfortable as I could, I was incredibly and understandably distracted from my teaching in every way. That was the best that I could do. So I decided that making a clean break from the school where I was working would be a healthy decision.

Luckily, for the following school year, in September 1983, an opportunity arose that began to take me away from the horrors that had just recently ended. I was offered a teaching position at a private school in Philadelphia to teach younger children (primary grades instead of Jr. High students). I was tremendously gratified.

The transition immediately did wonders for my emotional self. I was actively involved in a new environment with new people to meet. It was exciting. The students were wonderful. I very much enjoyed everything about it.

After two years in that environment, I felt like I was beginning to heal. But then I was approached by a group of parents looking for an interested educator about starting a brand new school program for their children totally from scratch. Philosophically, it was a dream-come-true. Emotionally it would be therapeutically exhausting by requiring that I focus 24/7 on the tasks at hand. I would be the Director, teacher, transportation coordinator, custodian, and secretary. It was just the kind of project that might be the vehicle to provide more balance in my still shattered life.

I could immerse myself in building a new program that I could create, and a program in which I believed. I could take my Pacific Oaks experience and skills, and test them out while being my own boss and evaluator.

Agreeing to make this effort made me proud of not letting my grief control my decision-making. So we opened Childworks Elementary School in September 1985 with 8 young boys in one small room in a church. With tremendous help from the parents, it lasted for five years after serving more than 25 children in grades K thru 5.

During this period of my life, I also found myself confiding in an old friend – Camp Galil. First, to help with the grieving process, I gathered three other Galil-connected friends to create the Chuck Albert Memorial Scholarship Fund to help needy families pay for their campers' to attend Camp Galil. I told myself that this was a powerful way to always keep Chuck in my consciousness, while allowing him some credit for doing the good deeds he would have wanted to do if he could. To date, the Chuck Albert Fund has aided dozens and dozens of families by helping to pay their camp tuitions. Second, I became the Registrar of Camp Galil and was responsible for finding and registering prospective campers. This was a second job that would surely keep my time and energy away from my sorrows.

Third, I volunteered to join the Camp Galil executive committee, which makes all of the essential decisions that facilitate all aspects of the camp business– hiring, budget, physical plant, etc. These responsibilities, along with my full-time teaching, offered me the chance to be and feel active, vital, confident, and worthy. All of these decisions helped me soothe away the grief that followed Chuck's death. They truly did help me fill the void that was left after my loss.

There was an axiom that creeped into my mind from time to time that was a tremendous help during the years after Chuck died. Similar to when he and I were children when we would share the details of events that we had had without the other one, I sometimes pretended that I actually had to live Chuck's life as well as mine. Helping kids go to Camp Galil was something he would have wanted. Writing my own set of songbooks to play his favorite songs on the guitar was another. Keeping his spirit alive helps me not miss him so much. And it helps me live the constructive life that we both had wanted for both of us.

In the early 1990's when I was in my early 40's, thoughts about my future became a higher priority for me. Childworks had been a tremendous accomplishment, but I was making very little money.

After a brief hiatus, I found the best job of my life where I would also earn an excellent salary. I was to be a teacher in the Abington School District's elementary program for Gifted Students. Since it included teaching a separate non-graded curriculum, it fit wonderfully with my teaching style. I was able to be creative in the way curriculum was offered, work with smaller groups, not give homework or tests, and be much more process oriented than in a regular classroom. I performed in that job for twenty years until I was able to retire. It was a blessing to be so happy in my professional life for such a long period of time.

Finally, I felt ready for a partner with whom to start a family. It had been very difficult for me to test my ability to care for someone new. I had so thoroughly learned the lesson that tremendous loss can occur in the blink of an eye. But it had been fifteen years since Chuck died. I was feeling ready for anything now. I wanted to put grieving behind me and accomplish the goals that I always had set out for my life.

It must have been fate one day when Camp Galil sent me to a conference in New York City. Emma, the woman registering the participants was very attractive, but "much too young for me." But although she was young, she decided that she was not too young.

We dated, and romanced, and discovered that we had much in common. The things we shared overwhelmed the wide age difference between us. We realized that our shared values and our complimentary personalities could create a love that would smooth each other's path into the future to attain what we both wanted in life.

Less than a year later, we were married at....you guessed it – Camp Galil. And now, twenty-three years later, we have two wonderful, intelligent, sensitive, empathetic children who have attended Galil for most of their childhood, including this passed summer. The three of them have lovingly and completely filled the emptiness that had been inside me.

I was lucky enough to have gone through my developmental years in a relationship with my brother that was tremendously and unconditionally close. When I lost him, I recognized that the power and strength that had been a part of our twin-ship was due to the support and caring we received from each other. That power had always been taken for granted.

When my twin died, it was tremendously wrenching and awful, and I grieved for many years. But I did not crumble. I honored his wishes to carry on. I honored his spirit to live a full and constructive life. I was able to accomplish starting and running a brand new school, helping to run a summer camp, finding a wonderful wife, and raising a beautiful family. Instead of falling apart, I know I made him proud.

RISK TAKING

Each person is largely a function of his or her given circumstances. We are not offered any choice about who our parents are, how smart we are, if we have red hair, if we are better at Math or at English, or if we hailed from America or Bolivia. I was not given the choice to be Chuck's twin, but being his twin gave me specific advantages.

As Chuck's twin, I was given the best possible support system – like at Robbie's house, for instance. And I know, as ironic as it may be, that the inner confidence gleaned from my twin-ship with Chuck is what provided me with the ability to overcome my grief and loss and remain (or even surpass) being the best me that I could be. The strength that allows me to write these words comes directly from my twin-ship.

I understand that it is documented that what most identical twins are most afraid of, is losing their identical twin. But I also understand the irony; that the tremendous, awful, pain and grief from losing a twin can eventually be overcome. And that is what happened to me…because of my ever-present connection to my brother.

Taking emotional risks is easier for me now. I don't get embarrassed very easily. I don't care who sees me cry. There is nothing else to lose once you have lost what you are most afraid of losing, and then survive. Now I know beyond doubt that a person can lose what is most dear, and have the strength to live healthily and constructively, even joyously, another day.

Somehow, within the deepest part of who I am, I have always known but never realized, that my life does not quite include many of the risks that most others' do. Now I understand that I have always carried a secret, even from myself. It was a secret that I couldn't quite hear until my twin brother was gone. But since then, I hear that secret very loud and very clear – that since I was conceived, I have never ever been alone…and I never will be.